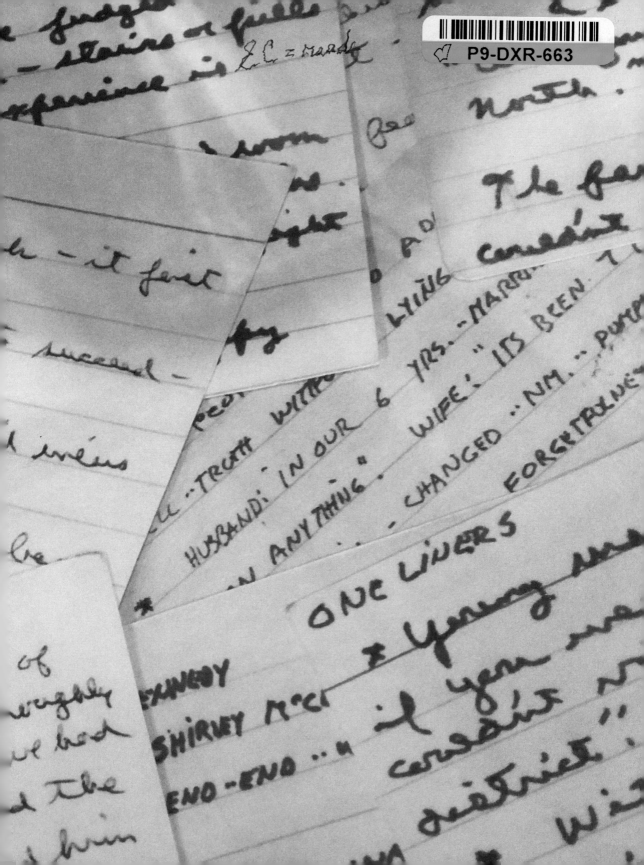

ℰℂ = marry

North.

The fee

LYING

comedie

6 YRS. – MARRI

WIFE: "ITS BEEN.

CHANGED .. NM .. PUMP

ANYTHING".

HUSBAND: "IN OUR

TRUTH WITH

FORGETFULNE

it feet

* ONE LINERS

succeed –

I Young

SHIRLEY McCl

it you

comedie's n

of

ME NO – END .. u

district "

Wis

# THE DAY
# THE PRESIDENT
# WAS SHOT

# THE DAY THE PRESIDENT WAS SHOT

The Secret Service, the FBI, a Would-Be Killer,
and the Attempted Assassination of Ronald Reagan

# BILL O'REILLY

Henry Holt and Company

NEW YORK

Henry Holt and Company, LLC
*Publishers since 1866*
175 Fifth Avenue, New York, New York 10010
mackids.com

Permission to use the following images is gratefully acknowledged
(additional credits are noted with captions): endpapers © Linnaea
Mallette / Dreamstime; case, pp. i, iii—Ronald Reagan Library;
pp. ii, vi–vii—Corbis; p. v—Mary Evans Picture Library; pp. xii—all
Michael Evans Portrait Collection / Ronald Reagan Library except
Nixon (Richard Nixon Library), Hinckley (Corbis), and Carter
(Jimmy Carter Library).
Maps on p. 143 by Gene Thorp.

Library of Congress Cataloging-in-Publication Data
Names: O'Reilly, Bill, author.
Title: The day the president was shot : the Secret Service,
    the FBI, a would-be killer, and the attempted assassination
    of Ronald Reagan / Bill O'Reilly.
Description: First edition. | New York : Henry Holt
    and Company, 2016.
Identifiers: LCCN 2015049781 (print) | LCCN 2015050719 (ebook) |
    ISBN 9781627796996 (hardcover) | ISBN 9781627797009 (ebook)
Subjects: LCSH: Reagan, Ronald—Assassination attempt,
    1981—Juvenile literature.
Classification: LCC E877.3 .O73 2016 (print) | LCC E877.3 (ebook) |
    DDC 973.927092—dc23
LC record available at http://lccn.loc.gov/2015049781

Our books may be purchased in bulk for promotional, educational,
or business use. Please contact your local bookseller or the Macmillan
Corporate and Premium Sales Department at (800) 221-7945 ext. 5442
or by e-mail at MacmillanSpecialMarkets@macmillan.com.

First edition—2016 / Designed by Meredith Pratt
Based on the book *Killing Reagan* by Bill O'Reilly and Martin Dugard,
published by Henry Holt and Company, LLC.
Printed in the United States of America by R. R. Donnelley & Sons
Company, Harrisonburg, Virginia

10  9  8  7  6  5  4  3  2  1

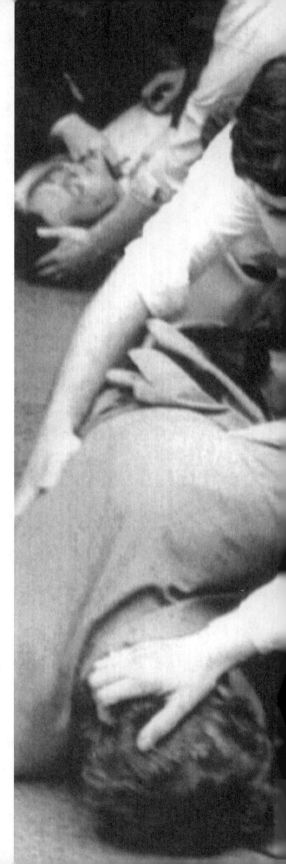

# CONTENTS

[NEXT PAGES] *The Oval Office, unoccupied, during Ronald Reagan's recovery
following the assassination attempt, April 1981.* [Ronald Reagan Library]

GETTING SHOT

# HURTS.

—Ronald Reagan in his diary,
reflecting on March 30, 1981

# A NOTE TO READERS

THE DAY THE PRESIDENT WAS SHOT is a story of courage, split-second decision making, superior training, and clear thinking. It is also a story of obsession and mental illness. These elements come together, of course, in the moment John Hinckley shoots the president, thinking he will impress a movie star, and a moment later when Agent Jerry Parr shoves Ronald Reagan into a limousine.

There are so many what-ifs in this heart-stopping story. What if John Hinckley had been identified as a threat when he was nabbed trying to get guns through airport security in Nashville? What if he hadn't been able to buy replacement guns? What if the president hadn't stopped to wave to fans who were standing close to him outside the hotel? What if Secret Service agent Timothy McCarthy hadn't spread his body around Reagan's and taken a bullet? What if Jerry Parr hadn't noticed the bloody handkerchief

★ x ★

Reagan lowered from his mouth? What if Washington, D.C., traffic had delayed driver Drew Unrue's arrival at the hospital?

Every single second counts.

The strength of character of the men hired to guard, drive, and protect Ronald Reagan began to save his life. The skill and speed of the emergency room staff, doctors, and nurses completed the task.

This book is a tribute to them—medical staff who work to heal each patient as if he or she is the president of the United States, and the men and women tasked with protecting world leaders. The best of them display the selflessness of true patriots.

GEORGE H. W. BUSH

ALEXANDER HAIG

CASPER WEINBERGER

RICHARD NIXON

JOHN WARNOCK HINCKLEY JR

MICHAEL DEAVER

JAMES BAKER III

EDWIN MEESE III

JIMMY CARTER

# KEY PLAYERS

## REAGAN ADMINISTRATION (PARTIAL LIST)

**George H. W. Bush:** Ronald Reagan's vice president, later the forty-first president of the United States, 1989–1993

**Alexander Haig:** secretary of state

**Ronald Reagan:** fortieth president of the United States, 1981–1989

**Casper Weinberger:** secretary of defense

## EXECUTIVE OFFICE OF THE PRESIDENT

**Richard Allen:** national security adviser

**James Baker III:** chief of staff

**James Brady:** press secretary

**Michael Deaver:** deputy chief of staff

**Edwin Meese III:** counselor to the president

**Larry Speakes:** deputy press secretary

## SECRET SERVICE (WHITE HOUSE DETAIL)

**Tim McCarthy:** Secret Service agent

**George Opfer:** head of the first lady's protective detail

**Jerry Parr:** head of the Presidential Protective Division

## OTHERS

**Benjamin Aaron:** surgeon who removed the bullet from Ronald Reagan's lung

**Leonid Brezhnev:** leader of the Soviet Union from 1964 until his death in 1982

**Jimmy Carter:** thirty-ninth president of the United States, 1977–1981

**Thomas Delahanty:** D.C. police officer

**Gerald Ford:** thirty-eighth president of the United States, 1974–1977

**Jodie Foster:** actress who starred in *Taxi Driver*

**Joseph Giordano:** surgeon, head of the trauma unit at George Washington University Hospital

**John Warnock Hinckley Jr.:** loner, wanderer, failed assassin

**Richard Nixon:** thirty-seventh president of the United States, the only one to resign from office, 1969–1974

**Nancy Davis Reagan:** Ronald Reagan's second wife

*Secret Service agents surround John Hinckley following his attempt to assassinate Reagan.* [Ronald Reagan Library]

IT TAKES JUST 1.7 SECONDS for John Hinckley to fire all six bullets.

The would-be assassin is immediately punched in the head by a nearby spectator, then gang-tackled by the crowd. Hinckley is buried beneath several hundred pounds of angry citizens as Secret Service agents try to take him alive. Ironically, their job now is to protect Hinckley with the same energy they devote to protecting the president.

As John Hinckley is subdued, three of his victims are fighting for their lives.

One of them is the fortieth president of the United States, Ronald Wilson Reagan.

# PART ONE

# THE ROAD
# TO THE
# WHITE HOUSE

# CHAPTER 1

# CONVENTION CENTER MUSIC HALL

## CLEVELAND, OHIO ★ OCTOBER 28, 1980 ★ 9:30 P.M.

FIVE MONTHS BEFORE the attempted assassination, Ronald Reagan strides to his lectern for the 1980 presidential debate. The former movie star and two-term governor of California is hoping to become president of the United States at the relatively advanced age of sixty-nine. His hair is black and his high cheekbones are noticeably rosy. At six feet one, 190 pounds, Reagan stands tall and straight, but his appearance does not intimidate: rather, he looks to be approachable and kind. With more than fifty movies and many television shows to his credit, Ronald Reagan is a familiar face to most Americans.

The governor's opponent is incumbent president Jimmy Carter. At five feet nine and 155 pounds, the slender Carter has the build of a man who ran cross-country in college. In fact, the president still makes time for four miles a day. Carter is a political junkie, immersing himself in every last nuance of a campaign. He has made a huge surge in the polls over the last month. Carter knows that

★ 4 ★

with one week until the election, the race is dead even. The winner of this debate will most likely win the presidency.

As both Reagan and Carter well know, the 1970s have been a brutal time for America. In 1974, President Richard Nixon resigned under suspicion of criminal activity in the Watergate affair. The unchecked growth of the Soviet Union's war machine and the American failure to win the Vietnam War have tilted the global balance of power. At home, inflation, interest rates, and unemployment rates are sky-high. Gasoline shortages have led to mile-long

*Cars line up at gas pumps in the 1970s.* [Mary Evans Picture Library]

*Shortly after Reagan is elected, President Carter invites the Reagans to tour the White House, November 20, 1980.* [Jimmy Carter Library]

lines at the pumps. And worst of all is the ongoing humiliation of fifty-two hostages still held in Iran after radicals stormed the American embassy in Tehran in 1979. A rescue attempt six months later failed miserably, resulting in the deaths of eight American servicemen. One week from today, when U.S. citizens go to the polls to pick a president, those fifty-two hostages will have spent exactly one year in captivity.

The United States of America is still very much a superpower, but an air of defeat, not hope, now defines its national outlook. The American public—Democrat and Republican alike—is in a patriotic mood. People long for a return to simple, straightforward American values.

The small theater in which the debate will unfold was built shortly after World War I, at a time when America had flexed its muscle on the world stage and first assumed global prominence. But tonight, there is a single question on the minds of many of the three thousand people in the auditorium and the 80.6 million watching on television:

Can America be fixed, or are the best days of the United States in the past?

# CHAPTER 2

# EVERGREEN, COLORADO

## OCTOBER 28, 1980

THIRTEEN HUNDRED MILES west of Ohio, in the city of Evergreen, Colorado, a twenty-five-year-old loner pays little attention to the debate. Instead, John Hinckley Jr. fixates on schemes to impress Jodie Foster, a young actress who starred opposite Robert De Niro in the movie *Taxi Driver*—a film Hinckley has seen more than fifteen times. Even though he has never met her, Hinckley considers Foster to be the love of his life and is determined to win her hand.

Hinckley's obsession with the seventeen-year-old actress is so complete that last month he temporarily moved to New Haven, Connecticut, to stalk her at Yale. Hinckley is a college dropout, unable to focus on his own studies, yet he had little problem attending a writing class. He slid poems and love notes into

*John Hinckley in a self-portrait, October 28, 1982.* [Corbis]

★ 9 ★

her dorm room, found her phone number, and, in a brazen move, called and asked Foster out to dinner. Shocked, she refused. So stunned was Foster by Hinckley's actions that she will not speak of the experience for years to come.

Now, nearly penniless and back with his parents, John Hinckley puzzles over how to make Jodie Foster change her mind. His plans are grandiose and bizarre. Hinckley has thought about killing himself right in front of her, or perhaps getting her attention by hijacking an airliner or assassinating someone famous.

The pudgy Hinckley, who wears his shaggy hair in bangs, has yet to see a psychiatrist for the schizophrenia that is slowly taking control of his brain. That appointment is in the future. But no amount of therapy will ever stop him from thinking about Jodie Foster—and the lengths he must go to to earn her love. Now, sitting in a small basement bedroom, Hinckley again considers suicide.

Bottles of prescription pills cover his nightstand. It will take a few more days to summon his courage, but Hinckley will soon reach for the container labeled VALIUM and gobble a deadly dosage.

But, true to form, John Hinckley will fail. He will wake up nauseated but alive, vowing to find some new way to impress Jodie Foster.

If killing himself is not going to work, then he will try to kill someone else.

*Jodie Foster and Robert De Niro in a still from the movie* Taxi Driver, *1976.*
[Mary Evans Picture Library]

# CONVENTION CENTER MUSIC HALL

## CLEVELAND, OHIO ★ OCTOBER 28, 1980

//////////////////////////////////////////////////////////////////

THE DEBATE DOES NOT GO well for President Jimmy Carter. His quiet, intellectual answers are overshadowed by Reagan's charm. Reagan can deliver a good line. His career in Hollywood has taught him poise under fire. He can convincingly express outrage, condescension, and certainty. He has memorized answers to the expected questions, of course. Both men have. But Reagan's polish tips the scale.

Watching from the side of the stage that night is Ronald Reagan's wife, Nancy. She can see that her husband is gaining confidence with every question. This gives her comfort, for Nancy was so afraid that her Ronnie would say something foolish that she initially opposed the debate. Nancy's opinion matters more to Reagan than any of his advisers'. They have been married twenty-eight years, and she has been a driving force behind his run for the presidency.

Reagan finishes the debate with a flourish. "Are you better off than you were four years ago?" he says earnestly into the television camera. "Is it easier for you to go and buy things in the stores than it was four years ago? Is there more or less unemployment in the country than there was four years ago? Is America as respected throughout the world as it was? Do you feel that our security is as safe, that we're as strong as we were four years ago? And if you answer all of those questions yes, why then, I think your choice is very obvious as to who you'll vote for. If you don't agree, if you don't think that this course that we've been on for the last four years is what you would like to see us follow for the next four, then I could suggest another choice that you have."

*Nancy Reagan in 1980.* [National Archives]

On Election Day, Ronald Reagan receives 50.7 percent of the popular vote and 489 electoral votes. Jimmy Carter receives 41.0 percent of the popular vote and just forty-nine electoral votes.

On January 20, 1981, Ronald Reagan is sworn in as the fortieth president of the United States.

John Hinckley Jr. now has a target.

# CHAPTER 4

# THE WHITE HOUSE

## WASHINGTON, D.C. ★ JANUARY 20, 1981

From the moment of his swearing-in, Ronald Reagan becomes the charge of the men in the Presidential Protective Division of the Secret Service. The group of crack agents is headed by Jerry Parr. And it seems amazing that the man who inspired Parr to become an agent is now the president of the United States. When Parr was nine, he went with his father to see the movie *Code of the Secret Service*, starring Ronald Reagan. Since joining the service, Parr has

*Ronald Reagan with his trusted agent, Jerry Parr.* [Associated Press]

*Movie poster for* Code of the Secret Service, *starring Ronald Reagan and Rosella Towne.* [Mary Evans Picture Library]

protected four vice presidents, many visiting heads of state, President Jimmy Carter, and now Ronald Reagan. Jerry Parr's job is to protect the president at all costs, including stepping into the path of an assassin's bullet.

# STUDIO CITY, CALIFORNIA

### MARCH 4, 1952 ★ 5 P.M.

/////////////////////////////////////////////////////////////

"I PRONOUNCE YOU MAN AND WIFE," says the reverend. Nancy Davis has succeeded in wooing her Ronnie.

This is his second marriage, and he brings two children with him. In 1938, when Reagan was making *Brother Rat*, he fell hard for his costar Jane Wyman. For a time they were Hollywood's golden couple. Their daughter, Maureen, was born in 1941, and in 1945

*Ronald and Nancy Reagan cut their wedding cake on March 4, 1952.*
[Ronald Reagan Library]

★ 17 ★

they adopted a baby boy they named Michael. But the marriage turned rocky after the death of a baby girl and the rise in Wyman's fame, and in 1948 they divorced.

Today, Ronald Reagan is dressed in a black wedding suit with a matching tie. Davis, who clutches a bouquet of white tulips, does not wear a wedding gown. Instead, she has chosen a gray wool suit with a single strand of pearls draped around her neck.

Nancy Reagan was born in New York City on July 6, 1921, as Anne Frances Robbins. Her mother was an actress, her father a traveling salesman. After they split up when she was just six, Nancy was sent to live with family in Maryland. A year later, her mother married a Chicago neurosurgeon named Loyal Davis, who adopted Nancy and gave her his name. Nancy studied dramatic arts at Smith College. In 1949, she traveled to Hollywood to pursue her dream of becoming an actress and was given a contract by MGM. Between 1949

[LEFT] *Nancy with her mother.* [Ronald Reagan Library]

[RIGHT] *Nancy in a publicity photo during her days as an actress.* [Mary Evans Picture Library]

and 1958, she made eleven feature films and went on to star in several TV shows.

In Ronald Reagan, Nancy sees a greatness that thus far has eluded him. She will dedicate her life to bringing this forth. Nancy Reagan possesses inner steel that her husband lacks. This quality will make her opinions indispensable to her husband. She will become his sounding board, tactician, and adviser, prodding and cajoling him to become the man only she believes he can be.

The power in their marriage will slowly shift until Nancy clearly has the upper hand.

Great marriages are sometimes made of this balance of temperament and strength.

//////////// **CHAPTER 6** ////////////

# ARDMORE, OKLAHOMA

**MAY 29, 1955** ★ **6 A.M.**

////////////////////////////////////////////////////////

THREE YEARS LATER, a twenty-eight-year-old mother of two is about to give birth to her third child. She and her husband are hoping that it will be a boy. They are affluent people, with a strong belief in the American dream.

If their child is indeed a boy, he will be named after his father, a deeply religious and highly successful oilman. There will one day be whispers that he is connected to the Central Intelligence Agency— whispers that will be scrutinized very closely.

But all of that is in the future as the hoped-for baby boy enters the world.

Two miles across the Oklahoma town, the modern Memorial Hospital is opening to the public. The baby could very well have been the first child delivered in this state-of-the-art facility. That would be a mark of distinction, if only in Ardmore. But Jo Ann, the mother, will deliver at Hardy Sanitarium, which will make the birth unique in another way. The opening of the new hospital means that Hardy, a two-story brick building that has been a vital part of Ardmore's fabric for fifty-four years, will close for good tomorrow. So, rather than being the first baby born in the new hospital, Jo Ann's baby will be the last born at Hardy.

So it is that John Warnock Hinckley Jr. is born in a small, obsolete hospital.

# CHAPTER 7

# STATE CAPITOL BUILDING

## ROTUNDA ★ SACRAMENTO, CALIFORNIA ★ JANUARY 2, 1967 ★ 12:11 A.M.

FIFTEEN YEARS AFTER THEIR MARRIAGE, Nancy's faith and determination have led to this moment. Despite making more than fifty films, Ronald Reagan has never known a moment of drama quite like the one he is experiencing right now. Dressed in a black suit with a narrow dark tie, he stands, head held high and feet planted twelve inches apart, like a conquering hero from the western movies he loves so much. His left hand rests on a Bible. A large bald man stands in front of him. A glance to his left shows Nancy Reagan prim and straight at his elbow, beaming. Television studio lamps light Reagan's face. "America the Beautiful" echoes in his head, thanks to a choir from the University of Southern California that serenaded him at the stroke of midnight.

This is Ronald Reagan's greatest moment, a time when at long last he gets to play the leading man. Just a year ago he was hosting yet another television show. Now he is the governor-elect of

*Reagan is sworn in as the thirty-third governor of California, 1967.*
[Ronald Reagan Library]

California. There's not a writer in Hollywood who could have scripted this any better.

Reagan raises his right hand and the swearing-in begins. One hundred fifty guests are closely watching him, waiting for the trademark smile and nod of the head that he has used to such populist effect while campaigning.

★　★　★

"Do you solemnly swear that you will support and defend the Constitution of the United States and the Constitution of the state of California against all enemies, foreign or domestic?" asks California Supreme Court Justice Marshall McComb.

"I do." Reagan's voice fills the rotunda, bouncing off the marble floors and the larger-than-life statue of Queen Isabella looking over him.

Reagan lets his gaze float out over the room. It is impossible not to be distracted. Men and women surround him, watching the proceedings with reverence. Several stand on tiptoe to better witness the historic moment.

These are Reagan's people. They also represent something of an anachronism. America is in turmoil, torn apart by the Vietnam War, a deep racial divide, drug use, and a sexual revolution. But in this room, at this moment, Reagan sees none of that conflict. Many filling this towering ceremonial space are as conservative as he is. The men wear crisp dark suits. Their hair is cut short, in sharp contrast to the shoulder-length locks so many young men are wearing these days. The women's knee-length dresses are a throwback to the more formal styles of the 1950s, nothing at all like the skimpy miniskirts popular at the time.

Reagan knows that some in the crowd might doubt his ability to lead, thinking of him as just an actor. He is also aware that his political views are at odds with current trends in American and California politics, thus making him a dinosaur in the eyes of many beyond the curved walls of this rotunda.

But on this cold January night, Ronald Reagan has a secret: despite what some may think of his abilities, the governorship will not be enough. Reagan hopes to be president of the United States one day.

*Ronald and Nancy Reagan around 1967 with Ron, born in 1958, and Patti, born in 1952.* [Ronald Reagan Library]

# EXECUTIVE RESIDENCE

## SACRAMENTO, CALIFORNIA ★ AUGUST 1972

//////////////////////////////////////////////////////////

Ronald Reagan is well into his sixth year as governor. He has achieved much as California's leader, cracking down on large student protests against the Vietnam War, balancing the budget so well that the state actually issued a tax rebate, and signing a bill that made abortions legal if the mother's physical well-being was in peril. In October 1971, Reagan traveled to Asia as a special representative of President Richard Nixon to calm foreign heads of state who were nervous about the thawing of relations between the United States and China.

And Nancy Reagan has prospered as California's first lady. She has come to enjoy the trappings of power, such as private jet travel, having an aide carry her purse, and the surprise friendship of Frank Sinatra. The famous singer has become a big supporter of Governor Reagan and a close friend of Nancy's.

*Ronald and Nancy Reagan at the victory celebration after his election as governor, November 8, 1966.* [Ronald Reagan Library]

*The governor at a press conference.* [Arthur van Court Collection / Ronald Reagan Library]

Even though her husband has stated publicly that he will not seek a third term as governor, Nancy is not about to give up a life full of perks and celebrity adulation. She is working behind the scenes to plan a presidential campaign. The time will come, Nancy believes, when her Ronnie will be ready for the big job.

# CHAPTER 9

# THE WHITE HOUSE

## WASHINGTON, D.C. ★ AUGUST 1973

THE LEADERS OF THE REPUBLICAN PARTY are shifting in Washington. Richard Nixon has been battling to stay in office. The Watergate scandal has been traced back to the White House. The men who planned and carried out the break-in at the headquarters of the Democratic National Committee have been sentenced to federal prison for burglary, conspiracy, and wiretapping. They have maintained a code of silence, saying that they operated without help.

Now another scandal shocks Washington, D.C.: the vice president of the United States has been taking bribes since his days as governor of Maryland. Spiro Agnew is accused of extortion, conspiracy, bribery, and tax fraud. Ultimately, he resigns on October 10, 1973.

So, even as he is under suspicion, Nixon has to choose a new vice president. Nancy hoped that Ronnie might be the choice, but he is third on the list after Gerald Ford and Nelson Rockefeller.

Reagan will have to wait.

*Henry Kissinger, Richard Nixon, and Alexander Haig listen to Gerald Ford (second from right) discuss his potential vice presidency.* [Richard Nixon Library]

# CHAPTER 10

# WASHINGTON D.C.

## AUGUST 9, 1974

From May 17 to August 7, 1973, Ronald Reagan and the nation were transfixed by 319 hours of televised testimony about the Watergate scandal. Because the crisis was considered so serious, the three television networks aired the Senate hearings without commercial interruption. The majority of historians, commentators, and viewers felt that the president's campaign activities had compromised the election process.

But Reagan had minimized the affair.

"They did something that was stupid and foolish and was criminal. It was illegal," he said. "Illegal is a better word than criminal because I think criminal has a different connotation. The tragedy of this is that men who are not criminals at heart and certainly not engaged in criminal activities committed a criminal or illegal act and now must bear the consequences."

As the months pass, the evidence that Richard Nixon engaged in a cover-up after the break-in grows. Nixon refuses to hand over to the Senate investigators secret tapes he had recorded in his office. Calls for his removal begin. In February 1974, the House of Representatives authorizes its Judiciary Committee to investigate grounds for impeachment. At the end of July, after the Supreme Court forces Nixon to release the tapes, the House Judiciary Committee adopts three articles of impeachment against the president.

Nixon resigns, effective today.

Before he leaves the White House, Nixon speaks to a large crowd of staff and supporters in the East Room. "Always give your best," he says. "Never get discouraged, never be petty; always remember, others may hate you, but those who hate you don't win unless you hate them, and then you destroy yourself."

Across the country, Ronald Reagan makes a statement to the press: "It is a tragedy for America that we have come to this, but it does mean that the agony of many months has come to an end."

As Nixon leaves the White House and steps into the helicopter that will fly him away from the presidency forever, Ronald Reagan is left to wonder if Gerald Ford will ask him to be the new vice president of the United States. Reagan tells reporters he would consider such a request "a call to duty."

But that call never comes.

*Nixon addresses his cabinet and staff before his departure, August 9, 1974.*
[Richard Nixon Library]

## CHAPTER 11

# DALLAS, TEXAS

**AUGUST 9, 1974 ★ 5 P.M.**

A s Reagan waits for a call in California, John Hinckley Jr. lies around, strumming his guitar. He is nineteen years old now, on summer break from college. He works in a local pizza joint called Gordo's, where he sweeps the floor and clears tables. Hinckley is putting pounds on his five-feet-ten frame. His Paul McCartney–type haircut frames his face, bangs sweeping low across the tops of his eyebrows. When he smiles, Hinckley's dull blue eyes come alive. Yet Hinckley rarely smiles, nor does he have any inclination to shed some of his expanding girth. He has little interest in physical fitness or presidential politics—or in anything, for that matter. While his older brother, Scott, is being groomed to run their father's oil company, and his sister is newly married and settling down, John has retreated into a world all his own. He speaks with a flat affect, and his gaze often lacks expression. His only comfort comes through music.

The truth is, John Hinckley is at a loss to explain what is happening in his brain. One out of every hundred people has some form of schizophrenia, a condition that causes the mind to distort reality. Hinckley is in the early stages of the brain disorder. If left untreated, his condition can tailspin into delusions and violent behavior that will become dangerous to Hinckley and to those around him.

His parents are currently building a new home in Evergreen, Colorado, a small mountain town populated largely by wealthy conservatives. They moved there from Dallas just a year ago, as John was beginning his freshman year at Texas Tech University. Having no friends in Evergreen, John Hinckley prefers to spend the summer in Dallas before heading back to school in the fall.

But Hinckley has no friends here, either. This is nothing new. Once, his high school classmates called Hinckley "as nice a guy as you'd ever want to meet." He was popular and well liked, a member of the Spanish Club, Rodeo Club, and Students in Government. But halfway through high school he abruptly stopped playing sports and taking part in school functions. His mother, Jo Ann, was heartbroken by the sudden change—and confused about why it happened.

John Hinckley is no longer one to experience happiness. It has been a long time since he has known that emotion. But here in his room, at least he is content. He listens to the Beatles and plays guitar, day after day after day. Today is a Friday. The president of the United States has just resigned. The world is in shock. Outside, the sun is shining on yet another baking-hot Texas summer afternoon. But John Hinckley does not notice. Within these walls, each day is just like the other. Friday might as well be Monday.

Hinckley's parents think themselves lucky that their son does not drink or take drugs. They are deeply religious Christians, and to know that their son is not violating biblical principles gives them some peace. So they leave him alone.

One day they will look back and realize that their son's withdrawal from society was not normal.

By then, it will be too late.

CHAPTER 12

# LOS ANGELES, CALIFORNIA

## APRIL 30, 1975

Ronald Reagan is now the former governor of California, having left office nearly four months ago. His successful economic policies as governor have led to an invitation to speak with British business leaders about ways to reduce the size of government and grow the economy. Giving speeches has become Reagan's primary occupation since moving from Sacramento back down to Los Angeles. He will make almost $200,000 this year traveling the world giving speeches. In addition, he has a weekly syndicated newspaper column, prepared by a ghostwriter, which goes out to 174 papers across the United States. And he personally writes the Saturday afternoon radio broadcast he delivers to more than 200 conservative stations nationwide.

Yet Ronald Reagan's mood is grim. And it is reflected in the mood of the country. Many believe America's decline began with the assassination of John F. Kennedy in 1963, continued through the antiwar protests of the late sixties, and then accelerated with the Watergate crisis in the early seventies. President Gerald Ford tried to stanch the bleeding by pardoning Richard Nixon for any and all crimes he may have committed while in office.

"My fellow Americans," Ford promised in his inaugural address, "our long national nightmare is over."

But it is far from over. And the outrage continues to grow. America, a nation built upon freedom and self-determination, has seen those principles twisted in a way that signals not some future form of greatness but imminent decay.

And no one seems to know how to stop it.

And now there is staggering news: Saigon, the capital of South Vietnam, has fallen to the North Vietnamese. American television cameras capture vivid images of American military, diplomatic personnel, and desperate Vietnamese citizens being hastily evacuated by helicopter. Thousands more Vietnamese mass around the embassy gates hoping to leave. After two decades, the Vietnam War finally ends in defeat for the United States.

*From 1961 until the end of the war in 1975, 58,204 U.S. military personnel were casualties of the Vietnam War. Here, a wounded soldier arrives at Andrews Air Force Base, Maryland, on March 8, 1968.* [Library of Congress]

*Vietnamese civilian evacuees stop over in Thailand as they wait for the next leg of their trip to the United States, April 29, 1975.* [National Archives]

# CHAPTER 13

# THE WHITE HOUSE

**WASHINGTON, D.C.** ★ **NOVEMBER 19, 1975** ★ **4:48** P.M.

///////////////////////////////////////////////////////

THE PHONE RINGS in the Oval Office. President Ford is meeting with his vice president, Nelson Rockefeller, and his chief of staff, Dick Cheney. Ronald Reagan is on the line. The president does not take the call.

Ford, a lifelong Republican who served in the navy during World War II, considers Reagan to be little more than a lightweight actor and a former Democrat. However, Reagan now represents the conservative vote, and this concerns the president. Rather than marginalizing his potential opponent, Ford has

*President Gerald Ford in the Oval Office, April 16, 1976.* [National Archives]

★ 43 ★

chosen to court Reagan. He has twice offered him a spot in his cabinet, telling the former governor that he can select almost any position he likes.

In addition, Ford asked Reagan to be part of a panel investigating allegations of domestic spying by the Central Intelligence Agency. All of this is an effort to prevent Reagan from running for president and splitting the Republican Party. Suspicious, Reagan keeps his distance, accepting the spot on the CIA panel to gain national political exposure but turning down any scenarios that would make him subservient to Ford. Finally, to gain conservative support, Gerald Ford strongly suggests that Rockefeller, leader of the moderate wing of the Republican Party, step down as vice president when the term ends. Rockefeller cooperates, and the path is now open for Reagan to become Ford's running mate in 1976.

But it is not to be. Reagan makes it clear that he has no interest in the secondary position.

He keeps Gerald Ford guessing as to whether or not he will challenge him. "I tried to get to know Reagan, but I failed," Ford will later write. "I never knew what he was really thinking behind that winning smile."

Today, Ford will find out. Reagan tries again at 4:57 P.M. This time, Ford picks up. Reagan is calling from his suite at the Madison Hotel in Washington, where he and Nancy have just checked in. In the morning at the National Press Club, Reagan tells Ford, he is going to announce his candidacy for president.

"I trust we can have a good contest," Reagan says.

# CHAPTER 14

# RAMADA INN

"WHEN YOU LEAVE THE PLATFORM, turn to your left," a Secret Service agent whispers to Ronald Reagan as he prepares to deliver his first speech as a presidential candidate. Reagan is in Miami. He and Nancy now have a Secret Service detail, offering round-the-clock protection against would-be attackers.

The whirlwind life of a presidential campaign has begun. The Reagans flew by chartered plane from Washington down to Florida this morning. After his speech at a Ramada Inn next to Miami International Airport, they will fly to Manchester, New Hampshire. Tomorrow it's on to North Carolina, and Illinois, and then California. This will be the Reagans' life for the next nine months, until the Republican National Convention in August. If they are lucky, they will get to continue the nonstop travel into November, when the national election is held. While the pace will be frantic, it will be well worth it. The ultimate goal for Ronald

*Michael Lance Carvin points a toy gun at Reagan.* [Corbis]

Reagan is to be elected president of the United States, and thus the most powerful man on earth.

In Miami, Reagan speaks for twenty minutes. At 2 P.M., he steps down from the podium and chooses to ignore the Secret Service's demand that he turn left. Instead, Reagan goes right, hoping to say hello to an old friend he has spied from the podium.

"What the hell do you think you're doing?" an authoritative voice says to Reagan as he walks up to the crowd of well-wishers.

Reagan is unafraid, eagerly shaking hands, working the crowd like the seasoned politician he has become. People smile and try to catch his eye. Suddenly, a dark-haired twenty-year-old man in a checked shirt stands just two feet in front of him, right arm extended, pointing a .45-caliber pistol at Reagan's chest.

Before Reagan can react, his Secret Service detail surges past him and wrestles Michael Lance Carvin to the ground. Reagan himself is shoved out of the way, the agents shielding his body with their own. The gun turns out to be a toy.

"I feel fine," Reagan later explains to the press.

"I hope it doesn't happen again," a startled Nancy Reagan tells the media. "I think you always have to keep it in the back of your mind."

Michael Lance Carvin is an admirer of Squeaky Fromme, who became famous when she tried to assassinate Gerald Ford. Ten days earlier, Carvin called the Denver office of the Secret Service to make death threats against Gerald Ford, Nelson Rockefeller, and Reagan. In April 1976, he will be convicted of seven felony charges relating to the threats and incident in Miami. Ordered to report to federal prison that June, Carvin will flee but be captured the next day by federal agents in Live Oak, Florida. After his release from prison in 1982, Carvin will lead a normal life, including getting married and landing a steady job, until 1998, when he will be arrested for making death threats against disc jockey Howard Stern. He will be sentenced to two and a half years in federal prison, though the term will be reduced to seven months.

★　★　★

Walking into a crowd is high on the list of actions the Secret Service would prefer that their principals, the people they protect, do not do. It is almost impossible to ensure a safe environment when the principal is surrounded by people.

While campaigning, candidates sometimes sit on the hoods of their cars, lean over protective barriers to kiss babies, or just walk away from their Secret Service handlers. It will not go unnoticed by the service that this candidate is a wanderer.

# KEMPER ARENA

**KANSAS CITY, MISSOURI ★ AUGUST 19, 1976**

////////////////////////////////////////////////////

N INE MONTHS LATER, Ronald and Nancy Reagan are hurrying through the twisting hallways and tunnels of Kansas City's Kemper Arena. The Republican National Convention is in its final moments, and the Reagans are on their way to the stage. The cheering of the crowd echoes down the corridors. Delegates from all over America are in a state of near bedlam. The moment Reagan shows his face, a collective roar shakes the arena.

Reagan is unsteady. "What am I going to say?" he asks Nancy.

He has not prepared a speech. The losing candidate is not supposed to speak at the convention. For as of last night, Ronald Reagan has officially lost the Republican nomination for president by a slender margin. Gerald Ford won with 1,187 votes; Reagan had 1,070. As he did so many months ago, Reagan made it clear that he would not accept the vice presidency if offered. So Ford did not offer.

The two candidates were neck and neck at the start of the convention. Ford won fifteen primaries, Reagan twelve, but the struggle to win delegates continued. Then Reagan committed a major blunder by announcing his running mate before the convention, selecting liberal Republican senator Richard Schweiker. This alienated Reagan's core conservative constituents. He tried to fix the error by suggesting that convention rules be changed to mandate that Ford also name his running mate early. The matter was taken before the Republican Party's Rules Committee, which voted it down. Ford won the nomination on the first ballot. Reagan will remain bitter about the defeat for years to come.

Gerald Ford's acceptance speech was masterful. Sixty-five times the crowd interrupted with applause. Watching Ford on television, Democratic nominee Jimmy Carter's campaign manager, Hamilton Jordan, parses no words in describing the apparent unity of the Republican party behind Ford: "It scares the shit out of me."

Now, in a display of party unification, the president has invited the Reagans onto the stage. Ford has the votes, but Reagan has the enthusiasm. Earlier in the evening, when Reagan first stepped into his box high up in the arena, his appearance had ignited a furor among the delegates.

"Viva!" Reagan's Texas supporters shouted.

*President Gerald Ford and First Lady Betty Ford (right couple) celebrate winning the nomination with Senator Bob Dole and his wife, Elizabeth (left couple), amid floating balloons at the Republican National Convention, Kansas City, Missouri.*
[Library of Congress]

*Ronald Reagan and President Ford at the Republican National Convention in Kansas City.* [Library of Congress]

"Olé!" responded his California followers, trying to outdo them.

Over and over, they chanted the words back and forth. The proceedings came to a halt, turning the convention into a massive party.

So Reagan must make a few remarks.

"Don't worry," Nancy tells him. "You'll think of something."

Reagan lets go of Nancy's hand and moves to the podium. The stage is a mob scene, with the Fords, Vice President Rockefeller, and new vice presidential candidate Bob Dole and his wife, Elizabeth, all crowded around. Reagan gropes for the words he will say even as he steps to the microphone, Nancy at his side.

Reagan praisies his party. "There are cynics who say that a party platform is something that no one bothers to read, and it doesn't very often amount to much. Whether it is different this time than it has ever been before, I believe the Republican Party has a platform that is a banner of bold, unmistakable colors with no pale pastel shades. We have just heard a call to arms based on that platform."

There was noise in the arena when Reagan began, but now it is hushed. Delegates hang on his every word.

There is no script to Reagan's speech, no notes. Reagan's impromptu address is dazzling. He veers away into his own deeply held political beliefs, until it is as if Ford were not there at all. Reagan speaks of the erosion of freedoms under previous Democratic administrations, the threat to the free economy, and "a world in which the great powers have poised and aimed at each other horrible missiles of destruction, nuclear weapons that can, in a matter of minutes, arrive in each other's country and destroy virtually the civilized world we live in."

Then Reagan articulates his thoughts on the peace and security of future Americans.

"Whether they have the freedoms that we have known up until now will depend on what we do here. Will they look back with appreciation and say, 'Thank God for those people in 1976 who headed off that loss of freedom'?"

Reagan is no longer a politician but a preacher. He stands not at a podium but at a pulpit. And Kemper Arena is his church. "This is our challenge, and this is why, here in this hall tonight, better than we've ever done before, we've got to quit talking to each other and about each other and go out and communicate to the world that we may be fewer in numbers than we have ever been, but we carry the message they're waiting for.

"We must go forth from here, united, determined," he concludes. "There is no substitute for victory."

The speech is about six minutes long, but that's all it takes for Republicans to see Reagan's vision, humanity, and charisma.

As Ronald Reagan waves good-bye to the crowd, it is plain to many across America that the Republican Party has nominated the wrong man for president.

Speaking to his campaign staff after the convention, Reagan makes it clear that this will not be his last bid for the presidency. "Nancy and I, we aren't going to sit back in our rocking chairs and say that's all for us."

# CHAPTER 16

# PACIFIC PALISADES, CALIFORNIA

## NOVEMBER 2, 1976 ★ 7:30 A.M.

Eleven weeks after Reagan electrified Republicans across America with his speech at the convention, Election Day finally arrives. It is a cool Los Angeles morning. Ronald and Nancy arise at 7:30, taking their breakfast of fresh orange juice, toast, and decaffeinated coffee at the kitchen table.

The Reagans walk a half mile to the longtime residence of Robert and Sally Gulick. The former World War II navy pilot and his wife have allowed their house to be used as a polling place for years, and it is here that the Reagans will cast their ballots.

All across America, voters are deciding who will lead them for the next four years: either incumbent president Gerald Ford or Democrat Jimmy Carter. It is a choice between the man who pardoned the despised Richard Nixon but kept the nation from further chaos and an outsider former governor, a devoted Southern Christian. Neither candidate inspires the nation. Watergate and the Vietnam War have made many Americans cynical. Today will see the lowest voter turnout since 1948.

★ ★ ★

Ronald and Nancy Reagan end Election Day 1976 by themselves in their home on San Onofre Drive. Since their son Ron left home to begin his studies at Yale University in Connecticut, the Reagans are empty nesters. On most nights, they watch an old movie and unwind before going to bed at eleven. But with all three television networks showing nothing but election returns, the Reagans cannot help but watch.

To them, neither presidential candidate offers the country the necessary ideology and passion. If only they had defeated Ford at the convention, this would have been their Election Day, and perhaps their night of triumph. Instead,

*Nancy and Ronald on horseback at Rancho del Cielo, their ranch high in the Santa Ynez mountains north of Santa Barbara, California.* [Ronald Reagan Library]

they sit alone in the house, looking out over the lights of Los Angeles and wonder—what if?

In the morning, the news is in: Carter narrowly beat Ford in the popular vote, 50 percent to 48 percent. He sealed his victory with 297 electoral votes, compared to Ford's 240.

*Jimmy Carter speaks to reporters at the White House, September 13, 1980.*
[National Archives]

# CHAPTER 17

# PACIFIC PALISADES, CALIFORNIA

## NOVEMBER 3, 1976

THE NEXT DAY is a new day.

As always, Ronald Reagan will spend a few hours in his study, writing his letters and speeches, laying the ideological groundwork to expand his conservative constituency.

But the story is different for Nancy Reagan. She has nothing at all to do. Shopping and socializing with her wealthy friends gets dull after a while.

So Nancy Reagan will see to it that her husband, Ronald Wilson Reagan, will become the president of the United States in 1980.

She will see to it.

# CHAPTER 18

# EGYPTIAN THEATRE

## HOLLYWOOD, CALIFORNIA ★ SUMMER 1976 ★ AFTERNOON

JUST FIFTEEN MILES from the home of Ronald and Nancy Reagan, John Hinckley sits alone in this aging movie palace, watching a film called *Taxi Driver*. It's a movie Hinckley will eventually see more than fifteen times.

The twenty-one-year-old drifter wears an army surplus jacket and boots, just like the film's main character, Travis Bickle. Hinckley's hair is now down to his shoulders, and his breath smells of peach brandy, another affectation he has picked up from Bickle, who is played with frightening intensity by the actor Robert De Niro.

The screenwriter of the film partly based the character of Bickle on Arthur Bremer, the would-be assassin of presidential candidate George Wallace in 1972. Bremer shot Wallace to become famous, to make a "statement of my manhood for the world to see." He had originally intended to kill President Richard Nixon but botched several attempts. The twenty-one-year-old Bremer attacked Wallace

JODIE FOSTER
a picture
sweater,
pleated mini

at a campaign rally in Laurel, Maryland, firing several shots at close range. One bullet lodged in Wallace's spine, paralyzing him for life. A Secret Service agent, a young campaign worker, and Wallace's personal bodyguard were also shot. Bremer was sentenced to fifty-three years in prison; he will be released after thirty-five.

But it is not De Niro who stirs the most emotion in John Hinckley. Instead, it is twelve-year-old Jodie Foster, who plays the prostitute Iris in the film. Jodie appears made up, her blond hair rolled into curls, lips painted a vivid red. Her character swears, smokes, and turns tricks with grown men. Hinckley is enchanted with her.

John Hinckley has come to Hollywood to be a star in his own right. He hoped to use his guitar skills to make his fortune, but that has not happened. His squalid accommodations at Howard's Weekly Apartments just off Sunset Boulevard have become a prison. "I stayed by myself in my apartment," he would later write of his months in Southern California, "and dreamed of future glory in some undefined field, perhaps music or politics."

The lonely Hinckley keeps to himself, living on fast food and slowly becoming convinced that Jews and blacks are the enemies of white men like himself. The more time he spends in Hollywood, the more Hinckley expands his circle of loathing. He now views the city of Los Angeles as "phony" and "impersonal."

*John Hinckley's poster and images of Jodie Foster, used as evidence at his trial.*
[Associated Press]

Isolated, Hinckley does not even keep in contact with his parents unless he needs money. Unwilling to finish his studies at Texas Tech or get a job, he would be homeless without their support. John and Jo Ann Hinckley are growing increasingly concerned about their son's behavior, but they support him financially, hoping that one day he will turn his life around and come back to Colorado. Hinckley gives them hope by writing that he is in a relationship with a woman named Lynn. But Lynn is not real.

There are more lies, such as the one about the rock music demo he fictitiously records. In reality, the only good thing in John Hinckley's life right now is up there on the screen at the Egyptian. *Taxi Driver* gives him hope and a sense of purpose. The fog of depression hanging over him lifts. Adopting the same manner of dress and behavior as Robert De Niro's character is empowering. In *Taxi Driver*, Hinckley sees a series of clues that will lead him to a better life.

The on-screen action shifts to an attempted political assassination. The scene shows Bickle intending to kill a presidential candidate to win the love of a woman. But the Secret Service foils Bickle's effort, and he slips away without firing a shot.

John Hinckley knows the next scene well. It is the final gun battle. Travis Bickle goes to rescue Jodie Foster's character from her pimp, who has hired her out to an aging mobster. A lone vigilante, Bickle blasts his way down the dingy hallway to where Iris is. Blood splatters the walls as the body count rises. The camera cuts to the terrified look on Iris's face as she hears the gunshots. It is her friend,

*A still from the movie* Taxi Driver, *starring Jodie Foster and Robert De Niro, 1976.*

[Mary Evans Picture Library]

Travis Bickle, who has come to save her. Despite her situation, she begs Bickle not to kill the mobster.

As the movie ends and the credits roll, Travis Bickle is a hero in the eyes of society—and in the eyes of John Hinckley.

And if Bickle can be a hero, then Hinckley can be a hero, too.

There are any number of reasons John Hinckley has fallen in love with that young girl up there on the screen. She is the one person the solitary Travis Bickle cares enough about to put his own life on the line for. And in real life, her name is Jodie, which is the nickname Hinckley's mother goes by. A delusion is beginning to take shape in his disturbed brain—that Jodie Foster might just be capable of falling in love with him. This condition is known as erotomania, a false but persistent belief that one is loved by a person, usually someone famous. It is often associated with mental illness.

The screen grows dark. John Hinckley steps out into the hot California sunlight. He heads down Hollywood Boulevard, passing the Walk of Fame. Without even noticing it, Hinckley strides right over the star Reagan received in 1960.

In addition to acquiring boots, an army fatigue jacket, and a newfound thirst for peach brandy, John Hinckley also keeps a journal, just like Travis Bickle. The only trait he has not borrowed from the taxi driver is a passion for owning guns.

That will soon change.

# THE WHITE HOUSE

## WASHINGTON, D.C. ★ APRIL 25, 1980 ★ 6:08 A.M.

/////////////////////////////////////////////////////////

JIMMY CARTER'S PRESIDENCY has had one setback after another. Catastrophic inflation has weakened Americans' buying power. Skyrocketing gas prices and long lines at the pump have shocked and angered the public. And now there is humiliation overseas.

The shortage of American gasoline was due in part to a yearlong revolution in Iran, which ended with the overthrow of the shah in January 1979 and installation of a new leader, Ayatollah Khomeini. With all the turmoil, Iran's oil production virtually ceased. Fearful of a repeat of the 1973 oil crisis, oil buyers bought up and stored the available oil, driving up prices 150 percent and further fueling inflation. To stop the inflation, the government has drastically raised interest rates, which are now as high as 20 percent, plunging the economy into recession.

In November 1979, Muslim militants stormed the U.S. embassy in Iran because of American support for the shah, who had been

admitted to the United States for cancer treatment two weeks earlier. The radicals took the embassy staff hostage and insisted that the shah be returned to Iran to stand trial for crimes committed during his thirty-eight-year reign. Fifty-three Americans have been held hostage for six harrowing months.

Carter authorized a daring rescue attempt.

Instead of celebration, though, there is disaster: eight American servicemen lie dead in the hot sands of the Iranian desert, their bodies burned beyond recognition. In a rush to flee without confrontation, their fellow soldiers left the dead behind. It is, perhaps, one of the greatest military humiliations in U.S. history.

Planned soon after the embassy take-over, Operation Eagle Claw was supposed to have sent an assault force of 118 U.S. soldiers into Tehran from the Persian Gulf to extract the hostages and evacuate them by air. Shortly after the force arrived

*Ayatollah Khomeini in Tehran, Iran, 1979.* [Corbis]

THE WHITE HOUSE

WASHINGTON

November 6, 1979

Dear Ayatollah Khomeini:

Based on the willingness of the Revolutionary
Council to receive them, I am asking two distinguished Americans, Mr. Ramsey Clark and Mr.
William G. Miller, to carry this letter to you
and to discuss with you and your designees
the situation in Tehran and the full range of
current issues between the U.S. and Iran.

In the name of the American people, I ask that
you release unharmed all Americans presently
detained in Iran and those held with them and
allow them to leave your country safely and
without delay. I ask you to recognize the
compelling humanitarian reasons, firmly based
in international law, for doing so.

I have asked both men to meet with you and to
hear from you your perspective on events in
Iran and the problems which have arisen between
our two countries. The people of the United
States desire to have relations with Iran based
upon equality, mutual respect, and friendship.

They will report to me immediately upon their
return.

                    Sincerely,

                    Jimmy Carter

His Excellency
Ayatollah Khomeini
Qom, Iran

at its Desert One staging area, however, the mission was aborted due to equipment problems. As the units prepared to depart Iran, a helicopter collided with a C-130 refueling plane. The subsequent explosion and fire killed eight airmen. The press was informed of the debacle at 1 A.M.

At 6:08 A.M., the president steps into the Oval Office. He sits at his desk in this great room and places a series of phone calls: to the first lady, Secretary of Defense Harold Brown, and Secretary of State Cyrus Vance. A news camera and microphone are brought into the room. The president straightens his tie. His speech lies before him on the desk.

Finally, at 7 A.M., Carter looks into the camera. He unemotionally explains his tactics to the nation, hoping his words will save his reelection campaign.

"Late yesterday I canceled a carefully planned operation which was under way in Iran to position our rescue team for later withdrawal of American hostages, who have been held captive there since November 4," he begins.

"Our rescue team knew, and I knew, that the operation was certain to be difficult and it was certain to be dangerous. We were all convinced that if and when the rescue operation had been

*Letter from President Jimmy Carter to Ayatollah Khomeini asking for the release of the Americans held hostage in Iran, November 6, 1979.* [Jimmy Carter Library]

*[NEXT PAGES] Reporters watch President Jimmy Carter on television making the announcement about the aborted attempt to rescue the U.S. hostages.* [Library of Congress]

commenced, that it had an excellent chance of success. They were all volunteers; they were all highly trained. I met with their leaders before they went on this operation. They knew then what hopes of mine and of all Americans they carried with them," Carter explains.

"It was my decision to attempt the rescue operation. It was my decision to cancel it when problems developed in the placement of our rescue team for a future rescue operation.

"The responsibility is fully my own."

★   ★   ★

Out of respect for the fifty-three captives, Carter has done little campaigning for reelection. He believes that remaining in the White House to deal with the crisis instead of traveling the campaign trail makes him look more presidential—and will ultimately win him another term.

That strategy is doomed to fail. And so is Jimmy Carter's presidency.

After his nationwide address on the Iranian disaster, Carter's job approval rating rises for a brief time but then settles back in the 30 percent range.

Ronald Reagan takes notice.

*A memorial service is held for the eight servicemen who were killed in the attempt to rescue the American hostages held in Iran. The U.S. flag is lowered to half-mast at the beginning of the ceremony, April 10, 1981.* [National Archives]

## CHAPTER 20

# NASHVILLE, TENNESSEE

### OCTOBER 9, 1980 ★ 12:02 P.M.

I T IS THREE WEEKS before Election Day when John Hinckley finally makes a plan to speed up his anticipated fame and glory. He will assassinate President Carter in order to impress Jodie Foster.

The four years since his first summer in Los Angeles have largely been a haze for John Hinckley. He continued to wander, shuttling from one state to another in an attempt to find himself, often returning to Texas Tech in Lubbock to take a few courses. His grades were Bs and Cs, but Hinckley has been in no hurry to graduate. At school, he woke up each morning and ate a half-pound hamburger from Bill's Lot-A-Burger. Once fastidious about neatness, Hinckley became a slob. He kept no food in his simple apartment, where a fine layer of dust from the local sandstorms and a pile of junk food bags covered the dining table.

In Lubbock, Hinckley regularly walked into Acco Rentals and talked football with owner Don Barrett. Other days he sat alone in silence by the pool at the Westernaire Apartments.

But recently, John Hinckley has developed a new passion. He's become enamored of Adolf Hitler and recently purchased a two-volume set of the German dictator's autobiography, *Mein Kampf,* for $30 at a Lubbock bookstore. Stories will eventually circulate that Hinckley joined the neo-Nazi National Socialist Party of America and wore the official brown uniform, with its swastika armband and storm trooper jackboots.

But neo-Nazi leader Michael Allen will later say that Hinckley was expelled from the party because he "wanted to shoot people and blow things up." Allen met Hinckley in 1978 and thought he was "a nut."

Allen will add that the party's leader in Texas had found Hinckley "uncontrollable" and preached violence openly.

★ ★ ★

Now John Hinckley spends what little money he has on handguns and airfare, following the president of the United States around the country, hoping to put a bullet in his head.

But today Hinckley reluctantly decided to delay the killing. He is running through the Nashville Metropolitan Airport, late for his plane. Over the last month, Hinckley has stalked Carter at appearances in Dayton, Ohio, and now Nashville, Tennessee. In Dayton, he got within six feet of Carter but did not shoot because, he says later, he was not in "a frame of mind in which I could carry out the act."

Today, in Nashville, Hinckley could not get close enough to squeeze off a shot. Security was too tight, so the would-be assassin decided to get out of town. Hinckley's oversized gray suitcase is clutched in one fist as he bears down on the security checkpoint. He bought his first handgun just a year ago, and now he owns several. Three of them—two .22-caliber pistols and one .38-caliber revolver—are inside his luggage. Hinckley is nervous. His heart races and he feels short of breath as he approaches the X-ray machine.

"I'm running late," he yells, doing his best to bluff his way through without having his suitcase scanned.

*John Hinckley poses in front of the White House, about 1981.* [Corbis]

The two security officers, Laura Farmer and Evelyn Braun, are unfazed. In fact, Braun thinks that the pudgy young man looks extremely suspicious. Rather than passing him through, she instructs Farmer to pay extra attention to the X-ray of Hinckley's bag.

John Hinckley reluctantly places the suitcase on the conveyor belt. The security officers notice that his hands are shaking.

Laura Farmer studies the video screen as it reveals the contents.

She signals to an airport security officer. John Lynch walks over and opens Hinckley's suitcase. Not only does he find the three handguns, but Hinckley is also carrying fifty rounds of .22-caliber hollow-point ammunition and a set of handcuffs.

Hinckley begins to argue, claiming that he is selling the guns, continuing to insist that he is late for his plane.

Officer Lynch ignores him. And places him under arrest.

Within an hour of his arrest in Nashville, John Hinckley stands before Judge William Higgins. The location is not a courtroom but a small office in police headquarters. He is being charged with illegal possession of a firearm.

A terrified Hinckley can only imagine what will happen next. He has never been in jail before. With President Carter just a few miles away at the Grand Ole Opry, it is logical that Judge Higgins or the FBI would question Hinckley about his guns and his intent. Even though it might appear to be a coincidence, the president's presence in Nashville demands that those questions be asked.

But on this day, John Hinckley is in luck. The FBI is so overwhelmed by Jimmy Carter's visit to Nashville that every last agent has been tasked with ensuring his safety. So there is no effective interrogation of Hinckley.

Judge Higgins's verdict is swift: John Hinckley will be punished to the maximum letter of the law. He is immediately ordered to pay a $50 fine, along with $12.50 in court costs. He also loses his guns.

John Hinckley walks out of Judge Higgins's courtroom a free man. He immediately returns to the airport, where he takes the next plane to New York.

# CHAPTER 21

# LOS ANGELES, CALIFORNIA

## NOVEMBER 4, 1980 ★ 5:35 P.M.

IN RONALD REAGAN'S MIND, defeating Jimmy Carter for the presidency was just a matter of time.

After accommodating George Bush with the vice presidential nomination at the Republican National Convention in Detroit, Reagan had a united party behind him. Reagan campaigned hard, crisscrossing the country, denigrating Carter's performance both at home and abroad. And he had plenty of ammunition: a bad economy and voter outrage about the Iranian debacle.

On November 4, 1980, the landslide is so great that Jimmy Carter concedes the election before the polls even close in California. He phones Ronald Reagan at home to give him the news.

Nancy Reagan answers the phone. Nancy calls her husband, who is in the shower, to the phone.

*Ronald Reagan, George H. W. Bush, and Howard Baker, the Republican leader of the Senate, at a campaign rally in front of the U.S. Capitol in Washington, D.C., September 15, 1980.* [Ronald Reagan Library]

"Standing in my bathroom with a wrapped towel around me, my hair dripping with water," Reagan will later recall, "I had just learned I was going to be the fortieth president of the United States."

# CHAPTER 22

# SMITHSONIAN NATIONAL MUSEUM OF NATURAL HISTORY

### WASHINGTON, D.C. ★ JANUARY 20, 1981 ★ 11:47 P.M.

R ONALD REAGAN STARES at the elephant in the room. It stands thirteen feet tall and measures twenty-seven feet from trunk to tail. The Fénykövi elephant is poised for battle in the center of the Museum of Natural History's festive rotunda. Its flanks are draped in patriotic red, white, and blue bunting, making it the very symbol of the Republican Party.

The other symbol of the party stands at a podium bearing the official seal of the president of the United States of America. Ronald Wilson Reagan gazes out over the hundreds of supporters dressed in formal attire who have come to celebrate his inauguration. He wears white tie and tails. Nancy Reagan is on his right, draped in a white satin sheath that took a team of dressmakers four weeks to embroider. This is the Reagans' ninth inaugural ball of the evening. And with midnight just minutes away, they still have one more to go.

Throughout the night, Ronald Reagan has remained vigorous. "I want to thank all of you," Reagan tells the crowd at the Smithsonian. His voice is growing hoarse after a long day and night of speeches, but though he is just weeks away from turning seventy years old, the new president shows no signs of fatigue. "Without you there wouldn't be this successful inaugural."

If Ronald Reagan's first day in office is any indication of what is to come, the United States of America is in for a far more upbeat presidency. He and Nancy spent last night at Blair House, the official guest house where the president-elect spends the night before the inauguration. The first couple is rested and ready to take full advantage of the celebration.

The Reagans have been in Washington for a week, adapting to the capital's routine after more than a year living out of suitcases on the campaign trail. Intense public scrutiny comes with their new life. A litany of personal facts is finding its way into the media. Given his age, many wonder about Reagan's health. Despite a medical history that includes a shattered femur suffered in a celebrity baseball game thirty years ago, the worst of his maladies right now are minor arthritis in his right thumb and chronic hay fever. He continues to work out each night, using a small exercise wheel before taking an evening shower. To some doctors, he is an amazing physical specimen for a man about to enter his eighth decade.

*President Reagan and Nancy Reagan pose before attending the inaugural balls in Washington, D.C., January 20, 1981.*
[Ronald Reagan Library]

*President-elect Ronald Reagan and his wife, Nancy, arrive in Maryland, December 15, 1980.* [National Archives]

The first event of the day was the formal transition of presidential power from one administration to the next.

Ronald and Nancy Reagan are driven from Blair House to the White House shortly before noon on Inauguration Day. There they are met by a somber Jimmy Carter and his wife, Rosalynn. Carter is exhausted from staying up all night in a last-minute attempt to free the hostages in Iran. This morning, per tradition, the two men ride together in a limousine for the two-mile journey to the Capitol for Reagan's swearing-in. They sit side by side in the

*President Carter and Rosalynn Carter receive President-elect Ronald Reagan and Nancy Reagan at the White House before the inauguration, January 20, 1981.*
[Ronald Reagan Library]

backseat but do not speak. Instead, each man looks out the window, waving to the crowds on his side of the limo. "He was polite," Reagan will later write. "He hardly said a word to me as we moved slowly toward the Capitol, and I think he hesitated to look me in the face."

Nancy Reagan and Rosalynn Carter are driven in a separate limousine, directly behind their husbands. Today is the end of a dream for Rosalynn, who grew up poor, her widowed mother taking in sewing to make ends meet. The differences between Rosalynn and

Nancy Reagan, with her debutante past and wealthy stepfather, are many. Rosalynn has attempted to be kind to Nancy throughout the transition, as her husband has been to Ronald Reagan. The Carters well remember the courtesies extended to them by the Ford family four years ago.

★ ★ ★

The Reagans have brought California weather with them. Tens of thousands of people stand in shirtsleeves and light jackets on this 55-degree day. The crowds stretch from the U.S. Capitol all the way down the National Mall to the Lincoln Memorial. American flags and red, white, and blue bunting seem to be everywhere, giving this day a jubilant sense of patriotism. Later on, once word gets out about the newly freed American hostages, yellow ribbons will be tied around every available tree, heightening the festive atmosphere.

★ ★ ★

Vice President George H. W. Bush is sworn in first. The choice of running mate was a savvy move on Reagan's part, as it was Bush who proved the toughest opponent during the 1980 Republican presidential primaries. A longtime party workhorse, the World War II fighter pilot has served as a congressman from Texas, director of the Central Intelligence Agency, and chairman of the Republican National

*By tradition, the sitting president and the president-elect share a ride to the inaugural ceremony in Washington, D.C.* [Ronald Reagan Library]

Committee. At six feet two, he stands an inch taller than Reagan and shares a similar athletic background. "Poppy," as he was nicknamed in his youth, is known for being a gentle yet tough man.

Bush now steps into the thankless role of vice president with the same aplomb he brought to each of his previous jobs. Reagan has plans to make great use of George Bush and his many skills in a manner heretofore unseen between a president and a vice president. Unlike Reagan, who can be privately aloof, Bush makes friends easily. He still keeps in touch with schoolmates and navy buddies he met decades ago. The same holds true in Washington, where Bush is deeply connected. Reagan's practical side will not allow him to let such qualities go to waste.

At the strike of noon, the new vice president steps away from the podium. It is now Ronald Reagan's turn to take the oath of office. He wears a gray vest and tie under his black suit as he places his hand on a Bible that once belonged to his mother. A poised Nancy Reagan is at his side, resplendent in a red dress. In what is a political first for Reagan, all four of his grown children are in attendance, standing with the other invited guests just behind him.

A burst of sunshine plays on Reagan's face as Chief Justice Warren Burger reads him the oath. "I, Ronald Reagan, do solemnly swear . . ."

*President Reagan stands at the podium to deliver his inaugural address, January 20, 1981.* [Ronald Reagan Library]

*Nancy gives a kiss to the newly sworn-in president.* [National Archives]

The oath takes just thirty seconds, and Reagan relishes repeating each phrase.

"May I congratulate you, sir," the chief justice says, reaching over to shake Reagan's hand. As a twenty-one-gun salute echoes off the Capitol walls, Reagan kisses his wife on the cheek. They turn together and look out on the thousands of Americans who have traveled to Washington to be here with them and witness this historic moment in person. Tonight there will be fireworks in the nation's capital. In New York, the Statue of Liberty will be bathed in

*Outgoing president Jimmy Carter congratulates Ronald Reagan.* [National Archives]

spotlights. For the next twelve hours, Ronald and Nancy Reagan will be celebrated with a dazzling succession of parades, parties, and speeches. Then, finally, will come the humbling moment when Ronald Reagan steps into the Oval Office for the first time.

As the most powerful man in the world, Reagan is preparing himself for the job by bringing in many political veterans. His chief of staff will be James Baker III, a fellow former Democrat who ran Gerald Ford's presidential campaign and then George H. W. Bush's four years later. Reagan likes that Baker is a no-nonsense manager known for his crisp analysis.

Reagan's deputy chief of staff, and the second man in what will become known as "the troika," or the three, is Michael Deaver, a member of his California gubernatorial staff whom both Ronald and Nancy prize for his loyalty.

And the third man upon whom Reagan will rely for advice in times of doubt is Edwin Meese III, an attorney who served as chief of staff during Reagan's California governorship. His official title is counselor to the president, but the forty-nine-year-old Meese's actual job goes much deeper than merely giving legal advice. He and Reagan know each other so well that Meese is often considered the president's alter ego. However, knowing that such a role can carry too much clout in the White House, Meese has made it a point to meet with Baker to define their roles. It is a balance of power that will be tested much sooner than either man is anticipating.

*President Ronald Reagan and Nancy Reagan wave during the inaugural parade.*
[Ronald Reagan Library]

*President Reagan holds a staff meeting on his first full day in the Oval Office with (standing left to right) Deputy Chief of Staff Michael Deaver, Chief of Staff James Baker III, Press Secretary James Brady, and (seated) Counselor to the President Ed Meese, January 21, 1981.*

[Ronald Reagan Library]

Thanks to his capable team, Reagan is confident that he can run the country. His first executive order lifts price controls on oil and gasoline, simultaneously setting in motion his personal idea of a free-market economy and making his many donors from the gas and oil industry billions of dollars richer.

"It is time for us to realize that we are too great a nation to limit ourselves to small dreams," he preaches in his inaugural address. "We're not, as some would have us believe, doomed to an inevitable decline. I do not believe in a fate that will fall on us no matter what we do.

"I do believe in a fate that will fall on us if we do nothing."

★   ★   ★

The last inaugural ball winds down well past midnight, but at nine the same morning, Ronald Reagan sits down at his desk in the Oval Office and scans the list of scheduled meetings. He wears a coat and tie, as he will each and every time he sets foot in this legendary work space.

Reagan is firmly in command. Or so it seems to those around him.

Little does he know the violence that lies ahead.

# CHAPTER 23

# STAPLETON INTERNATIONAL AIRPORT

## DENVER, COLORADO ★ MARCH 7, 1981 ★ 6 P.M.

JOHN HINCKLEY SHUFFLES OFF the United Airlines flight from Newark, New Jersey, eyes glazed from fatigue and face unshaven. He has spent a week on the East Coast in yet another futile attempt to win Jodie Foster's love. "Dear Mom and Dad," the twenty-five-year-old wrote in a note just seven days ago, "your prodigal son has left again to exorcise some demons. I'll let you know in a week where I am."

But Foster once again rejected Hinckley, and yesterday at 4:30 A.M. a broke and incoherent Hinckley phoned his parents, begging for a ticket to fly home. He is unaware that Jodie Foster has given his love letters to the Yale University campus police, who are currently launching an investigation into his whereabouts.

Hinckley is among the last passengers to disembark. His fifty-five-year-old father, Jack, is waiting. His mother has not made the drive into the city from Evergreen because she is so distraught about

*A note from John Hinckley to Jodie Foster, marked as an exhibit for his trial.* [Corbis]

her son that she has spent the day crying. The entire Hinckley family has been devastated by John's behavior. His sister, Diane, and older brother, Scott, want their parents to place John in a mental hospital. "He just keeps going down," Scott Hinckley told his father yesterday. "John doesn't seem like he can cope anymore."

But coping is the least of it. If Jack and Jo Ann Hinckley were the sort of people to pry, they would find a box for a handgun, bullets, and paper targets in the shape of a man's torso hidden inside a small green suitcase in their son's bedroom closet. But they do not believe in snooping into their son's belongings, nor his personal business. They have no idea why John impulsively flew to New York City, and they certainly have no knowledge about the grandiose scheme to court Jodie Foster.

This does not mean that Jack and Jo Ann are completely hands-off. It was through their urging that their troubled son has begun seeing a Colorado psychiatrist about his failing mental health. Dr. John Hopper, however, does not see anything greatly wrong with John Hinckley. In their sporadic sessions together over the last five months, Hopper has seen no signs of delusions or other symptoms of mental illness. John Hinckley trusts Hopper enough to confess that he is "on the breaking point" mentally, but rather than be alarmed, the psychiatrist thinks him a typical socially awkward young man who exaggerates his obsessions. Hopper treats Hinckley by attaching biofeedback electrodes to his forehead and thermometers to his fingers in an effort to teach him relaxation techniques.

Relaxation, Hopper believes, is vital to curing Hinckley.

The psychiatrist also believes that Jack and Jo Ann Hinckley are mostly to blame. He believes they coddle their son, not holding him accountable for his behavior. They allow him to live at home and don't force him to find a job. So Hopper has encouraged them to draw up a contract to set in motion the wheels of John Hinckley's independence. By March 1 he is to have a job; by March 30 he is to move out of the house. "Give John one hundred dollars," Dr. Hopper told the Hinckleys, "and tell him good-bye."

Technically, John Hinckley has remained true to the contract. He beat the deadline for finding employment, landing a menial position with the local Evergreen newspaper. But he walked away from that job when he flew to New York. Now, in the busy Denver airport, a heartbroken Jack Hinckley must perform a most gut-wrenching act of parenting: he must tell his son good-bye.

Jack Hinckley guides John to an unused boarding gate. "Have you eaten anything?" he asks.

"I bought a hamburger in New York, and ate again on the plane," John replies.

They sit down. Jack is direct, telling his son that he is no longer welcome in their home. "You've broken every promise you've made to your mother and me. Our part of the agreement was to provide you with a home and an allowance while you've worked at becoming independent. I don't know what you've been doing these past months, but it hasn't been that. And we've reached the end of our rope."

John Hinckley is shocked. Even at age twenty-five, he is so accustomed to having his parents solve his problems that his father's words stun him.

Jack presses $200 into John's hands. "The YMCA is an inexpensive place to live," he says softly.

"I don't want to live at the Y."

"Okay, you're on your own. Do whatever you want to do."

The two men walk to the airport garage, where John Hinckley parked his car six days ago. Jack Hinckley has brought along antifreeze, knowing that the car has a leaky radiator. He adds the antifreeze and gets the car running.

"Then I watched him drive slowly away down the ramp," Jack Hinckley will later write of that moment.

"I did not see my son again face to face until we met in prison."

★   ★   ★

About three weeks later, John Hinckley parks in his parents' driveway. He has been living at a dive called the Golden Hours Motel, thirty minutes away in Lakewood.

Jack is at work, so it is Hinckley's mother who answers the door. John is flying to California to start his new life, and Jo Ann Hinckley has agreed to drive him to the airport.

Mother and son barely speak during the hour ride to Stapleton. She does not want him to leave, but she forces herself to stick with what she and her husband call "the plan."

She parks in front of the Western Airlines terminal. Jo Ann violates the plan by giving John $100. "He looked so bad and so sad and so absolutely in total despair," she will later recall. "I thought he would take his own life."

But John Hinckley's flirtation with suicide has passed. He has a very different form of killing on his mind. "Mom," he tells her, saying good-bye once and for all to his former life, "I want to thank you for everything you've ever done for me."

Jo Ann Hinckley knows something is wrong. Her son never speaks with such formality. But the plan must be obeyed, so she overrules her intuition and does nothing to stop John from leaving. If not for the plan, the course of history might have been changed.

"You're very welcome," Jo Ann tells her son. Her voice is intentionally cold because she knows she will start sobbing if she lets down her guard. Then, without a kiss or hug or even a handshake, she drives away.

Little does she know, in his luggage her son is carrying an RG 14 .22-caliber pistol.

It has become a vital part of his plan.

## CHAPTER 24

# WASHINGTON, D.C.

### MARCH 1981

RONALD REAGAN IS HAVING TROUBLE with the Russians.

On February 24, Soviet leader Leonid Brezhnev gave a three-hour speech in front of a Communist Party gathering in Moscow and proposed that he and Reagan meet to mend relations. The seventy-four-year-old Brezhnev is a short, overweight man with enormous, bushy eyebrows who has ruled his nation for seventeen years. During that time, Reagan and his advisers feel, Brezhnev has pursued a ruthless path of aggression against the United States and the West, secretly building a nuclear arsenal and military that now exceeds those of America and NATO. This is a violation of several treaties to keep world peace. Although the United States and the Soviet Union have adopted a policy of détente, a relaxing of tensions between the two superpowers, Reagan sees the Soviet Union still acting as an aggressor, with America usually acceding to its demands to keep the peace.

It is a policy that Ronald Reagan abhors.

"It has been a long time since an American president stood up to the Soviet Union," he says to his son Michael. "Every time we get into negotiations, the Soviets are telling us what we are going to have to give up in order for us to get along with them, and we forget who we are."

When Reagan says as much to reporters, the Soviets are listening.

Reagan thinks Brezhnev was bluffing in his speech, pretending to seek peace. The Soviet leader wanted to bully the untested American president.

*Leonid Brezhnev* [Mary Evans Picture Library]

But Ronald Reagan is in no mood to be bullied—certainly not by Leonid Brezhnev.

In a televised news interview, Reagan responds to a question about negotiating with the Soviet Union: "It is rather foolish to have unilaterally disarmed, you might say, as we did by letting our defensive margin of safety deteriorate, and then you sit with the fellow who's got all the arms. What do you have to negotiate with?"

Brezhnev furiously dictates a nine-page letter to Reagan. "The Soviet Union has not sought, and does not seek military superiority," he seethes. "But neither will we permit such superiority to be established over us. Such attempts, as well as attempts to talk to us from a position of strength, are absolutely futile. . . . To attempt to win in an arms race, to count on victory in an atomic war—would be dangerous madness."

# CHAPTER 25

# THE WHITE HOUSE

## WASHINGTON, D.C. ★ MARCH 25, 1981

SINCE REAGAN RECEIVED THE LETTER from Brezhnev on March 6, the president's advisers have debated and drafted responses. On March 25, a draft is sent to the Oval Office. After reading it, Ronald Reagan flies by helicopter to Marine Corps Base Quantico, where he will spend two hours on horseback, reflecting.

The draft on his desk is not what he wants. The president decides to send it back to the State Department, asking for a revision.

A few days later, his request is fulfilled. But once again, it is not the letter Reagan has in mind.

The date is March 30, 1981.

Ronald Reagan has been in office sixty-nine days.

But no letter will be written that day.

Instead, an act of pure evil intervenes.

PART TWO

MARCH 30, 1981

| Lab Number | Evidence | Location |
|---|---|---|
| | Items from dumpster in trash area of Park Central Hotel (3rd Floor) | |
| Q49 | Forty-four (44) pieces of torn yellow tablet paper. | Washington Field Office (WFO) |
| Q50 | One Eastern Airlines Boarding Pass | WFO |
| Q51 | One (1) torn piece of paper possibly a portion of a ticket. | WFO |
| | Item received from reception desk of Park Central Hotel | |
| Q52 | ████████████████████ | WFO |

(b)(7)(c):(b)

### Items From Tan Suitcase located In Room 312 (#1 through #28)

1. Rugger long sleeve pull over shirt, red and white horizontal stripes (tag torn out).  WFO

2. Dark green long sleeve button up shirt, size Large.  WFO

3. Blue long sleeve button up shirt "BIG MAC J.C. PENNEY"  WFO

4. Light blue long sleeve button up shirt (J.C. PENNEY 16 1/2-33).  WFO

5. Short sleeve pull over shirt dark blue and beige horizontal stripes (tag torn out).  WFO

6. Dark blue and gold pull over shirt with short sleeves. OP on left sleeve (tag torn out).  WFO

H-16

# PARK CENTRAL HOTEL

## WASHINGTON, D.C. ★ MARCH 30, 1981 ★ 9 A.M.

JOHN HINCKLEY IS HUNGRY. HE turns off the *Today* show in his budget hotel room and steps out on the corner of 18th and G Streets in downtown Washington, D.C. The sky is overcast. A light rain settles on Hinckley's well-worn beige jacket as he strolls three blocks to the K Street McDonald's.

He did not sleep well last night, troubled by how to play out his Jodie Foster obsession once and for all. Money is also on his mind. Hinckley is almost broke. After spending $47 on his room last night, he has just $130 left to his name. This is barely enough for a ticket back home to Denver, but John Hinckley does not care. He will never return to that home again.

On his way to breakfast, Hinckley stops at the local Crown Books. He browses, looking for literature about his two favorite topics: the Beatles and political assassination.

*A list of evidence from the FBI report on John Hinckley and the assassination attempt.*
[Federal Bureau of Investigation]

But little interests Hinckley this morning. He leaves the bookstore, crosses the street to McDonald's, orders an Egg McMuffin, and sits down in a booth to plan his day. Unlike most Washington tourists, Hinckley does not envisage hours of sightseeing. Instead, he will either take the train to New Haven to shoot himself dead in front of Jodie Foster, or he will murder Massachusetts senator Ted Kennedy and add his own name to the list of notorious assassins who have stalked and killed a member of that political dynasty.

If that target is not available, he might enter the U.S. Senate chamber, trying to kill as many lawmakers as possible. And there is one other scenario in Hinckley's mind: assassinating President Ronald Reagan.

No matter which of the four schemes he chooses, Hinckley has the means to pull it off. Nestled within his large suitcase back at the Park Central are his snub-nosed pistol and forty-three bullets.

Hinckley sits alone in the McDonald's for an hour. He cannot make up his mind. Shortly before eleven, he walks back to the Park Central, stopping along the way to buy today's edition of the *Washington Star*.

# THE WHITE HOUSE

## WASHINGTON, D.C. ★ MARCH 30, 1981

//////////////////////////////////////////////////////////////////////

AT THE SAME MOMENT, two blocks away in the White House, President Ronald Reagan is concluding a ceremonial fourteen-minute meeting in the Cabinet Room with a group of Hispanic leaders. It has been a long morning of meetings, beginning with a breakfast for his political appointees in the Blue Room at 8:30 and then a fifteen-minute session with his top advisers. More meetings and a conference call round out the morning, each with a revolving cast of administration officials. Among them is James Brady. As Reagan's press secretary, Brady deals with the media, using wit and intelligence to get the president's message to the public. Brady's sense of humor and candor impressed the president and have made him popular with the Washington press corps.

[NEXT PAGES] *Ronald Reagan and James Brady in the Oval Office, January 20, 1981. In frames 10A and 11A, Jerry Parr monitors the visitors near the doorway.*
[Ronald Reagan Library]

Brady is hoping to tighten his bond with Ronald Reagan in the coming months by spending time with him. This afternoon, Reagan is due to give a short speech at the Washington Hilton, but since the president will not be taking questions from the press, Brady does not have to accompany him.

Ronald Reagan spends thirty minutes alone in the Oval Office, revising his upcoming speech. The audience will be liberal union members who oppose his politics, but Reagan is confident he can win them over with his Irish charm.

Finally, at 11:24 A.M., Ronald Reagan slips out of the Oval Office and walks along the colonnade next to the Rose Garden, then takes the elevator upstairs to his private residence. There, the president changes into a new blue suit before sitting down to a lunch of soup and fruit—without Nancy today, since she is attending a luncheon in Georgetown.

*President Reagan walks down the White House colonnade that connects the Residence and the West Wing.* [Ronald Reagan Library]

# CHAPTER 28

# PARK CENTRAL HOTEL

## WASHINGTON, D.C. ★ MARCH 30, 1981

WHILE THE PRESIDENT EATS LUNCH, John Hinckley takes a shower. He is deep in thought as the water beats down on him. The morning paper lists the president's schedule, showing that Ronald Reagan will be giving a speech at the Washington Hilton Hotel this afternoon. This presents Hinckley with a dilemma: should he murder the president or should he kill himself in front of Jodie Foster? He has already decided against murdering Ted Kennedy or shooting up the Senate chamber. Now, with his options down to just two, Hinckley soaks under the water, trying to make up his mind.

"I was thinking, should I go over to the Hilton with my little pistol and see how close I could . . . well, see what the scene was like," he will later explain.

Hinckley rinses, then turns off the shower.

His mind is made up: he is going to the Hilton.

He gets dressed in a pair of simple trousers, a shirt, and ankle-high boots. His wallet contains $129 in cash, along with two library cards, a Texas driver's license, a chess club membership card, and folded magazine photos of Jodie Foster. There is no guarantee he will fire his gun this afternoon, but if he does get close enough to squeeze off a round, John Hinckley wants Jodie Foster to know he is doing it for her. He sits down at a small wooden desk and composes a letter to his beloved:

*Dear Jodie,*

    *There is a definite possibility I will be killed in my attempt to get Reagan. It is for this very reason that I am writing you this letter now.*

    *As you well know by now I love you very much. Over the past seven months I've left you dozens of poems, letters and love messages in the faint hope that you would develop an interest in me. Although we talked on the phone a couple of times, I never had the nerve to simply approach you and introduce myself. Besides my shyness, I honestly did not wish to bother you with my constant presence. I know the many messages left at your door and in your mailbox were a nuisance, but I felt that it was the most painless way for me to express my love for you.*

    *I feel very good about the fact that you at least know my name and know how I feel about you. And by hanging around your dormitory, I've come to realize that I'm the topic of more than a little conversation, however full of ridicule it may be. At least you know that I'll always love you.*

*Jodie, I would abandon the idea of getting Reagan in a second if I could only win your heart and live out the rest of my life with you, whether it be in total obscurity or whatever.*

*I will admit to you that the reason I'm going ahead with this attempt now is because I just cannot wait any longer to impress you. I've got to do something now to make you understand, in no uncertain terms, that I'm doing all of this for your sake! By sacrificing my freedom and possibly my life, I hope to change your mind about me.*

*This letter is being written only an hour before I leave for the Hilton Hotel. Jodie, I'm asking you to please look into your heart and at least give me the chance, with this historical deed, to gain your respect and love.*

*I love you forever,*
*John Hinckley*

He adds the time—12:45 P.M.—to the date and places the letter in an envelope. He leaves the letter in his suitcase so that investigators will find it should he succeed in murdering the president.

John Hinckley stands and removes the pistol from his suitcase, along with boxes of ammunition. Several types of bullets soon litter his bedspread. Hinckley has the choice of normal round-nosed bullets or hollow-point bullets, which expand on impact to create a large hole in the target. He also has six rounds of an especially brutal ammunition designed to explode on impact, sending bullet fragments tearing through a target like shrapnel.

Appropriately, these bullets are known as Devastators.

He chooses them.

Armed and dangerous, Hinckley takes a cab for the short ride to the Washington Hilton. A small crowd of journalists and spectators awaits Ronald Reagan's arrival. A padded black rope has been

*An FBI specialist describes a Devastator bullet at a press conference.* [Corbis]

*The Washington Hilton* [Library of Congress]

hung across the sidewalk by hotel security to keep the crowd a safe distance from the president.

Pistol snug in his jacket pocket, John Hinckley joins the crowd. The time is 1:46 P.M.

# CHAPTER 29

# WASHINGTON, D.C.

## WHITE HOUSE

The White House detail of the Presidential Protective Division prepares for the president to leave the White House grounds. Several vehicles are readied and lined up in order. There will be sixty-six Secret Service agents at the event. Many are already at the Hilton scanning the rooms and hallways for explosives, checking the staff and reporters for clearance papers, and working with hotel security and city police to establish a safe perimeter for the president's entrance and exit.

The Secret Service knows this hotel well. Presidents have gone in and out safely more than a hundred times since 1972.

*A 1972 presidential limousine, a Ford Lincoln Continental.* [Wikimedia]

# CHAPTER 30

# WASHINGTON HILTON HOTEL

## MARCH 30, 1981

AT ALMOST THE EXACT TIME Hinckley arrives at the Hilton, Ronald Reagan gets into his 1972 Lincoln Continental. The Secret Service calls the car Stagecoach and the president Rawhide, references to the westerns he loves. Secretary of Labor Raymond Donovan joins him in the backseat.

Several vehicles carrying members of Reagan's staff, White House physician Dr. Daniel Ruge, and many Secret Service agents make up the motorcade. It is a 1.3-mile drive to the Hilton.

Press Secretary James Brady is also in the caravan. At the last moment, he decided to make the trip to hear what Reagan will say.

At 1:51 P.M., the presidential motorcade arrives at the Hilton.

★ ★ ★

John Hinckley stands in the crowd of spectators behind the security rope, watching the motorcade approach. The main entrance of the Hilton is behind him. The president will not enter through that door. Instead, he will use the canopy-covered VIP entrance just forty feet away.

The assassin feels an unlikely burst of excitement at the prospect of seeing Reagan in person. Hinckley pats the pistol in his right pocket. Ample time at the rifle range has prepared him for what is to come. He knows the .22-caliber Röhm must be fired at close range for peak accuracy, and the spot where he now stands is well within the pistol's optimal range of ninety feet.

Hinckley surveys the scene. More than two dozen Secret Service agents are ready to protect the president. Hotel security and

*U.S. Secret Service members watch from a rooftop during the presidential inauguration in Washington, D.C., on Jan. 20, 2005.* [U.S. Air Force photo by Scott H. Spitzer, Released/ National Archives]

Washington police also crowd around the Hilton, including two police officers facing the crowd on the other side of the security rope. Hinckley notices that there are some Secret Service agents on nearby rooftops.

Suddenly, President Reagan's limousine glides past the security rope and comes to a halt just outside the VIP entrance. An agent steps out of the front passenger seat and hustles to open Reagan's door on the right rear side of the vehicle. Quickly, the president emerges into the afternoon drizzle, taking a moment to wave to the crowd.

D.C. police officers Herbert Granger and Thomas Delahanty are working the security rope and should be facing the crowd for signs of trouble. Instead, they crane their heads to the left to see the president.

This is the perfect time for John Hinckley to shoot.

But he does not. Hesitating, he responds to the president's wave with a wave of his own.

"He was looking right at me and I waved back," Hinckley will recall. "I was kind of startled."

In a blink, Reagan is inside the building.

★　★　★

The time is 2:02 P.M. The president is introduced by Robert Georgine, the forty-eight-year-old head of the Building and Construction Trades Department of the AFL-CIO union. Reagan bounds onto the stage to the strains of "Hail to the Chief" and then launches into his speech.

Ronald Reagan enjoys public speaking. It comes easy to him. He begins, as usual, with a joke.

★   ★   ★

John Hinckley hears laughter coming from the ballroom. He has left the security rope to step inside the Hilton and wander around the lobby. "Should I? Should I?" he asks himself repeatedly, feeling the weight of his gun in his pocket. He is having second thoughts about killing Ronald Reagan. If he were to leave right now and go back to his hotel, nobody would be the wiser. He could burn his letter to Jodie Foster and slide the gun back into his luggage. Rather than die in a hail of Secret Service bullets or spend the rest of his life in prison, John Hinckley could simply walk away. "I just wasn't that desperate. I just wasn't that desperate to act," he will later state. "Also, it was raining. And I wasn't going to stand around in the rain."

Hinckley makes up his mind: he will go back to the spectator area and wait. If Reagan does not appear in ten minutes, Hinckley will leave.

The time is 2:19 P.M. Ronald Reagan has five minutes left in his speech.

★   ★   ★

*Reagan speaks at the Washington Hilton, March 30, 1981.* [Ronald Reagan Library]

Philips Gallery

Meanwhile, less than two miles away, Nancy Reagan is lunching at the Georgetown home of Michael Ainslie. The president of the National Trust for Historic Preservation is hosting the first lady and the vice president's wife, Barbara Bush, after their brief morning tour of modern art at the Phillips Collection.

But Nancy Reagan suddenly tells Secret Service agent George Opfer she is not feeling well. It's nothing specific, just a general feeling of anxiety. The worried first lady says her good-byes and is driven back to the White House at 2:20 P.M.

★ ★ ★

John Hinckley is now back in the spectator area outside the Hilton. He works his way to the very front of the crowd, so that the black rope presses against his belly, and his right shoulder leans against the front wall of the hotel. Three Washington police officers stand on the other side of the rope, facing him. Hinckley later remembers that they, as well as Secret Service agents, turned away from the crowd when President Reagan appeared.

The would-be assassin notices immediately that the Secret Service has moved Ronald Reagan's limousine to facilitate an easier departure from the hotel. Rather than being parked just outside the VIP entrance, it is now standing so close to the security rope that the right rear bumper almost touches the spectator area. Ronald

*A photo diary of Nancy Reagan's morning: touring the Phillips Collection and lunching at Michael Ainslie's home. The photographer also captures moments of private conversation between Nancy and Barbara Bush.* [Ronald Reagan Library]

Reagan will enter the Lincoln not forty but just ten feet away from where John Hinckley now stands.

All at once, Hinckley is jostled. Reporters are pushing to get in a better position to ask Reagan questions. Hinckley is outraged, shouting to the other spectators that the media should not be allowed to push their way to the front of the crowd. But it soon becomes clear that the press is providing a vital distraction.

Everyone is paying attention to the media.

No one is paying attention to John Hinckley.

★   ★   ★

Ronald Reagan finishes his speech at 2:24 P.M. The applause is polite, which disappoints him, for it is not the robust ovation he was hoping to hear. "Speech not riotously received," he will later write in his diary. "Still it was successful."

As part of his daily routine, Reagan places a checkmark next to each item on his agenda once it is concluded. The speech to the Building and Construction Trades having just earned its checkmark, the president leaves the stage and immediately follows his Secret Service escort to the car. Press Secretary James Brady stands just inside the VIP door with Michael Deaver as Reagan approaches. Secret Service agents rush past Brady, taking up their positions near the limousine. Agent Tim McCarthy is tasked with opening the right rear door for Reagan.

James Brady steps out of the VIP entrance before his boss, walking next to Deaver. The president has chosen not to take questions, so Brady will speak to the reporters himself. "Deal with them," Deaver says tersely as he heads toward the car that will ferry him back to the White House.

James Brady steps closer to the crowd as Ronald Reagan walks out the hotel door. Secret Service agent Jerry Parr is one step, about eighteen inches, behind. He moves slightly to Reagan's right. If something were to happen within the first few steps outside the VIP door, Parr will immediately force Reagan back inside the safety of the hotel.

The first fifteen feet to the presidential limousine pass without incident. Parr is no longer thinking about pulling Reagan back; now he is focused on moving the president forward into the car.

Agent McCarthy opens the right rear door of the limo. Agent Parr moves behind the president. Brady stands ten feet from him, walking quickly to the security rope to greet the press. McCarthy stands ready to close the door behind Reagan, unsure if the president will linger to wave to the crowd before getting inside the car.

The time is 2:27 P.M.

★　★　★

John Hinckley sees Ronald Reagan clearly. He also sees the crowd of agents—"body men" in Secret Service code—accompanying Ronald Reagan. Hinckley notices James Brady moving toward the rope line. Things are happening very quickly.

The president raises his right arm and waves to the crowd. A woman calls out from the spectator area as if she knows him.

*President Reagan waves to the crowd outside the Washington Hilton. Jerry Parr, in a tan coat, follows closely behind.*
[Ronald Reagan Library]

A friendly Reagan motions in her direction. Normally the president wears a bulletproof vest when appearing in public, but the walk from the hotel door to the car is so short that the Secret Service did not think he needed it today.

John Hinckley braces his right arm against the rough stone wall, dropping his hand into his pocket. Quickly, he pulls out the gun.

Later, Hinckley testifies that his head was telling him, "Put the gun away."

But he does not.

Tomorrow, the worldwide media will begin investigating this loner and describe him as a deranged gunman, as if he has no idea what he is doing. But

John Warnock Hinckley is a cold-blooded man who has trained himself in the art of murder.

Just as he has done so many times at the firing range, Hinckley grasps the butt of the pistol with two hands for maximum stability. He bends his knees and drops into a shooter's crouch, then extends both arms and pulls the trigger.

The first bullet hits James Brady square in the head, just above the left eye. He falls face-first to the ground, his blood dripping through a sidewalk grate.

The second shot strikes D.C. police officer Thomas Delahanty in the neck, lodging against the spinal column. He falls to the ground in agony, screaming for a priest.

The third shot goes wild, hitting no one.

*Thomas Delahanty and James Brady fall to the ground.* [Ronald Reagan Library]

*During the shooting, with Officer Thomas Delahanty lying in the foreground.*
[National Archives]

The fourth bullet strikes Secret Service agent Tim McCarthy in the chest. He, too, falls to the sidewalk, seriously wounded, a bullet lodged behind his liver.

The fifth shot bounces off the limousine.

The sixth also hits the Lincoln but ricochets—piercing Ronald Reagan's body under his left arm. The bullet enters his lung, coming to rest just one inch from his heart.

*[LEFT] President Reagan is captured in three stills as he is shot.* [Associated Press]

# CHAPTER 31

# WASHINGTON HILTON HOTEL

### MARCH 30, 1981 ★ 2:27 P.M.

AT THE SOUND of the first bullet, Agent Jerry Parr grabs Reagan by the belt and pushes him down and behind the limo's armored door. Parr has not seen the assassin or glimpsed the gun. It is simply the sound of gunfire that sets him in motion. By instinct he and the other agents cover and evacuate, shielding the president's body with their own while getting him away from danger as quickly as possible.

Another agent thrusts both men hard into the limo and slams the door behind them. They land in a heap, with Parr on top. Reagan's face hits the backseat; his chest hits the hump between the seats. An intense wave of pain shoots through his body.

Ten seconds after the first shot, the limousine is speeding away.

*Despite law enforcement's best efforts to protect the suspect, news cameras join the huddle.* [Corbis]

# CHAPTER 32

## WASHINGTON, D.C.

### MARCH 30, 1981

"Jerry," the president cries, "get off. I think you broke one of my ribs."

Parr doesn't have time to be solicitous. He needs to get the president to safety immediately. "White House," he barks at Agent Drew Unrue, who sits at the wheel.

Parr climbs off the president. Neither man knows that Ronald Reagan has been shot. But as Reagan tries to sit up, he is "almost paralyzed by pain."

"Were you hit?" asks a concerned Parr.

"No, I don't think so," Reagan responds.

Parr runs his hands over the president's shoulders, chest, and head. He sees no sign of blood. Reagan can barely sit up, his face ashen. He begins pressing his left arm against his chest as if having a heart attack. He coughs hard, sending a stream of bright red blood onto a handkerchief in his hand.

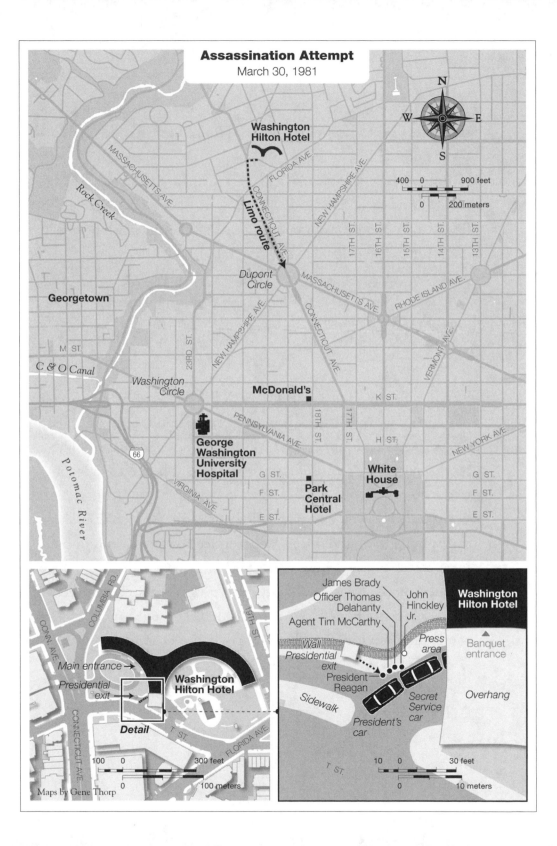

# Assassination Attempt
## March 30, 1981

Washington Hilton Hotel

Limo route

FLORIDA AVE.

CONNECTICUT AVE.

NEW HAMPSHIRE AVE.

MASSACHUSETTS AVE.

17TH ST.

16TH ST.

15TH ST.

14TH ST.

13TH ST.

400    0    900 feet

0    200 meters

Rock Creek

Georgetown

Dupont Circle

MASSACHUSETTS AVE.

RHODE ISLAND AVE.

NEW HAMPSHIRE AVE.

CONNECTICUT AVE.

VERMONT AVE.

M ST.

C & O Canal

23RD ST.

Washington Circle

McDonald's

K ST.

18TH ST.

17TH ST.

NEW YORK AVE.

66

PENNSYLVANIA AVE.

George Washington University Hospital

G ST.

H ST.

White House

G ST.

VIRGINIA AVE.

Park Central Hotel

F ST.

F ST.

Potomac River

E ST.

E ST.

CONN. RD.

COLUMBIA RD.

19TH ST.

Main entrance →

Presidential exit →

Washington Hilton Hotel

Detail

T ST.

FLORIDA AVE.

CONNECTICUT AVE.

100    0    300 feet

0    100 meters

Maps by Gene Thorp

James Brady

Officer Thomas Delahanty

Agent Tim McCarthy

John Hinckley Jr.

Washington Hilton Hotel

Press area

Banquet entrance

Wall

Presidential exit

President Reagan

Sidewalk

Secret Service car

Overhang

President's car

T ST.

10    0    30 feet

0    10 meters

"You not only broke a rib," he tells Parr as the presidential limousine races to the safety of the White House, "I think the rib punctured my lung."

Reagan tastes blood and tells Parr that he might have cut his mouth. The agent looks closely, seeing that the blood on Reagan's lips contains numerous air bubbles, which is the sign of a lung injury.

"I think we should go to the hospital," Parr tells Reagan.

"Okay," Reagan answers, still believing that Parr broke his rib.

It takes Ronald Reagan's limousine three minutes to get to the hospital.

★   ★   ★

At the same time, in the third-floor White House solarium, Secret Service agent Opfer calmly enters the room and interrupts Nancy Reagan's conversation with the White House's chief usher. "There was a shooting," Opfer informs the first lady. "The president is going to the hospital."

Distraught, Nancy Reagan is led out of the White House as a car is brought around. Her Secret Service code name is Rainbow, in reference to the many colors of her fiery personality. But there is no evidence of that on display right now. She is quiet and terrified. When her two-vehicle motorcade gets caught in Washington gridlock on its ten-block journey, she becomes frustrated. "I'm going to get out and walk," she yells. "I need to walk. I have to get there."

Traffic begins to flow.

★   ★   ★

The president walks through the emergency room doors under his own power, but his knees begin to buckle and he has to be carried to a trauma bay. "I feel so bad," Ronald Reagan tells the nurse who quickly begins cutting clothes off the president's body. "I feel really awful. I can't breathe."

This is the first indication that something is very wrong with Ronald Reagan. At first, doctors believe Ronald Reagan may die. An attempt to take his blood pressure has not yielded a reading, meaning that his heart is barely pumping.

All around Reagan, the emergency room is a frantic scene of doctors, nurses, and well-armed Secret Service agents. Dr. Joseph Giordano, a surgeon who heads the hospital's trauma team, is inserting a clear plastic chest tube into Reagan, hoping to drain the blood from his chest cavity. "This better go well," Dr. Giordano tells himself as he slices open the president's skin.

"He was seriously injured," Dr. Giordano will later remember. "He was close to dying."

★   ★   ★

Fifteen minutes after leaving the White House, Nancy Reagan's limousine pulls up to George Washington University Hospital. As soon as the vehicle stops at the emergency entrance of the gray cinderblock building, she sprints toward the emergency room. Waiting at the door is Deputy Chief of Staff Mike Deaver.

"He's been hit," Deaver tells her.

"But they told me he wasn't hit," replies a shocked Nancy Reagan. "I want to see my husband," she pleads.

★　★　★

Ronald Reagan is a seventy-year-old man who has just suffered a devastating trauma. Not only was he shot, but he was thrown into a car, where his chest slammed hard into a hump between the two seats. His body may not have the ability to endure much more.

Reagan is conscious throughout the procedure. Once he is stabilized, the next step will be surgery to remove the bullet. Spotting Jerry Parr just before being wheeled to the operating room, Reagan shows the first sign that he might make it: "I hope they're all Republicans," he tells the Secret Service agent who saved his life less than thirty minutes ago.

Later, in the operating room, Dr. Giordano hears about the quip. "Mr. President," the surgeon—a lifelong Democrat—tells Reagan, "today we are all Republicans."

★　★　★

A pained but lucid Ronald Reagan is being prepped for surgery. He lies on the gurney and looks up to find Nancy gazing down at him. She is unsteady. She has never seen her husband so white. A nurse removes the president's oxygen mask from his mouth. "Honey," he tells her, hoping that a joke will erase the fear from her face, "I forgot to duck."

Nancy fights tears as she bends down to kiss him. "Please don't try to talk," she whispers.

Later, Nancy will remember this moment with sadness and fear. "I saw him lying naked with strangers looking down at his naked body, and watching the life ebb from him, and as a doctor's daughter, I knew that he was dying," she will recount to her friends.

But Ronald Reagan is experiencing another reaction. He will later write of the joy this moment gives him. "Seeing Nancy in the hospital gave me an enormous lift. As long as I live, I will never forget the thought that rushed into my head as I looked up into her face. Later, I wrote it down in my diary: 'I pray I'll never face a day when she isn't there. Of all the ways God has blessed me, giving her to me is the greatest and beyond anything I can ever hope to deserve.'"

Reagan is wheeled into surgery. Nancy clings to the bed's handrail, walking with the team of doctors and the surgically gowned Secret Service agents who will accompany her husband into the operating room.

"Who's minding the store?" Reagan asks Ed Meese as the gurney passes the White House counselor.

At the double doors leading into the surgery center, Nancy is told she cannot accompany her husband any farther.

The time is 3:24 P.M.

All she can do is wait.

★  ★  ★

At 4 P.M., Ronald Reagan lies unconscious on the operating table. A rib spreader pulls his fifth and sixth ribs apart, allowing Dr. Benjamin Aaron to clearly see inside Reagan's chest. The seventh rib is indeed fractured, because the bullet glanced off it. More troublesome is the blood filling the chest cavity. The president has lost half of his body's total blood supply. Tubes running into Reagan's body fill him with new blood, antibiotics, and hydration fluid.

Dr. Aaron's goal is to remove the bullet from Reagan's body, but there is a big problem. While he can trace its path through the half-inch-wide hole it has left in the lung, he cannot find the .22-caliber round.

Using his fingers, Dr. Aaron reaches inside the president's body and feels for the bullet, delicately working around Reagan's slowly beating heart. "I might call it quits," the frustrated surgeon says.

★  ★  ★

Frustration also reigns one mile away at the White House.

Deputy Press Secretary Larry Speakes is holding a press conference on live television. All across America, millions are glued to their sets as regular programming has been interrupted. A somber America awaits news about the severely wounded Ronald Reagan.

*As news of the president's condition filters into the White House from the hospital, David Gergen (top), Larry Speakes (middle), and Alexander Haig (bottom) address the press.* [Ronald Reagan Library]

Situation Rm

But if viewers are looking for reassurance, Speakes's words do not provide it. When he is asked if the president is in surgery, he replies, "I cannot answer that question at this time."

The press conference is unsettling people more than reassuring them.

Normally the vice president would speak to the nation, but at this moment, Vice President Bush is on a plane over Texas heading back to Washington. The plane does not have secure phone or radio connections to the White House, so Bush can't control the sensitive events that are unfolding.

Instead, General Alexander Haig barges into the briefing room. Knees buckling, voice cracking, and grasping the podium so hard his knuckles turn white, Haig proclaims his authority to the nation on live TV.

"As of now, I am in control here in the White House."

The secretary of state, who has long sought to expand his power, appoints himself temporary president.

Constitutionally, the general is incorrect; Speaker of the House Thomas "Tip" O'Neill Jr. is next in line.

One floor below where the press conference is taking place, members of Ronald Reagan's cabinet huddle in the White House Situation Room, horrified at Speakes's inarticulateness and Haig's blustering. Even worse, they know something that the press secretary

*The Situation Room meeting on the assassination attempt and chain of command.*
[Ronald Reagan Library]

does not: the Soviets are taking advantage of the uncertainty surrounding Reagan's condition by moving submarines alarmingly close to America's East Coast. Secretary of Defense Caspar Weinberger has ordered America's bomber crews to go on standby alert. With the president now unconscious and Vice President George Bush in the air somewhere over Texas, the authority to respond to the Soviet threat falls to Weinberger.

Fearing the worst, National Security Adviser Richard Allen has ordered that the nuclear launch codes that could begin World War III be brought to him. They now sit on a desk here in the Situation Room, concealed beneath a small pile of papers.

★ ★ ★

Nancy Reagan is desperately praying. She sits in the hospital chapel, along with the wives of Press Secretary James Brady and Secret Service agent Tim McCarthy. All three of their husbands are currently in surgery. The women are unaware that the media will soon report that James Brady is dead.

*Secretary of State Alexander Haig takes control.*
[Ronald Reagan Library]

The women are not alone in this small second-floor sanctuary. White House Chief of Staff James Baker kneels in prayer, and Mike Deaver and Ed Meese join the vigil. They are as close to the president as any group of advisers could be, and the wait is agonizing.

★   ★   ★

Finally, at 5:25 P.M., thanks to a set of X-rays that show the bullet's location, Dr. Aaron feels the dime-size chunk of metal. The surgeon carefully squeezes the bullet out from Reagan's lung with his fingertips.

"I've got it," he tells the surgical team. A member of the Secret Service steps forward to take the bullet as evidence.

Dr. Aaron now turns his attention to cleaning the surgical areas and closing the president's chest.

Finally, at 6:46 P.M., an unconscious Reagan is wheeled from the operating room. The greatest crisis has passed, but danger remains.

Within an hour, Reagan is awake, though groggy. A breathing tube in his throat makes it impossible for him to talk, so he scribbles a note to his nurse. "If I'd had this much attention in Hollywood, I'd have stayed there."

★   ★   ★

Twenty miles away at Andrews Air Force Base, the plane carrying Vice President George Bush has finally touched down on the runway. Bush had been slated to give a speech in Austin, Texas. When news came that Reagan was shot, he returned to Washington. His return marks the end of Alexander Haig's self-declared three-hour reign as leader of the free world. And while Haig was legally wrong to declare himself in charge, his blunt behavior has had one positive effect: Soviet forces are backing down.

In the White House Situation Room, National Security Adviser Richard Allen quietly places the nuclear launch codes back in their special briefcase.

# CHAPTER 33

# METROPOLITAN POLICE HEADQUARTERS

## WASHINGTON, D.C. ★ MARCH 30, 1981

WITHIN A HALF HOUR of the shooting, John Hinckley sits in a D.C. police interrogation room. He complains that his wrist might be broken; there are also cuts and bruises on his face from being shoved to the concrete sidewalk. But for the most part Hinckley is calm.

Hinckley rode in with two Secret Service agents who had been assigned to protect the president. But it is the job of the police to arrest and question him, and homicide detective Eddie Myers is trying to do just that.

"How do you spell *assassinate*?" Myers absentmindedly asks a fellow officer during the questioning.

"A-s-s-a-s-s-i-n-a-t-e," Hinckley answers, smirking.

The police don't know much yet except Hinckley's name and address. They are mystified about his motives. Their primary

*John Hinckley is driven away after the attempted assassination.* [Corbis]

concern right now is to determine if he acted alone or is part of a conspiracy. To find out more, they have to get him to open up.

About 5 P.M., Hinckley's case is transferred from the local police to the FBI, and he is moved to the bureau's Washington field office. FBI agent George Chmiel and Secret Service agent Stephen Colo settle down to interrogate Hinckley. Chmiel gets him to say that he worked alone, and Colo discovers Hinckley's warped fascination with Jodie Foster.

For the next year, the FBI investigates every detail of John Hinckley's life to create a case against him. And Hinckley's lawyers do as much work interviewing his psychiatrists and doctors to establish the case that he was insane.

# CHAPTER 34

# GEORGE WASHINGTON UNIVERSITY HOSPITAL

**WASHINGTON, D.C. ★ MARCH 31, 1981 ★ 10 A.M.**

IT IS NOT UNTIL MORNING that Ronald and Nancy Reagan are allowed to see each other again. She has spent a long night alone in the White House, sleeping on his side of the bed, hugging one of her husband's T-shirts to feel his presence. At 10 A.M., Nancy enters the intensive care unit with Patti and Ron, who have made the trip to Washington upon hearing of the shooting. Although Michael and Maureen, children from Ronald Reagan's first marriage, have

*An anxious Nancy Reagan arrives at the hospital, bringing jelly beans for her husband.* [Associated Press]

traveled to the hospital also, they are not ushered in until Nancy's children have their moment.

Ronald Reagan is oblivious to any sibling rivalry. He sees his family and is deeply moved. His breathing tube has been taken out, allowing him to joke and visit with Nancy and his children. He knows the shooting has changed his life forever.

"Whatever happens now I owe my life to God," he will write in his diary, "and will try to serve him in every way I can."

*President Reagan appreciates a "Get Well Soon" poster from the White House staff. The poster also acknowledges the other three men who were injured.* [Ronald Reagan Library]

*President Reagan leaves the hospital with Jerry Parr and Nancy on his right and Patti on his left.* [Ronald Reagan Library]

# PART THREE

# MOVING ON

# U.S. CAPITOL

**WASHINGTON, D.C.** ★ **APRIL 28, 1981** ★ **7 P.M.**

//////////////////////////////////////////////////////////

T HE PRESIDENT WHO WAS NEARLY KILLED is bathed in
applause. Members of Congress leap to their feet in bipartisan
support of the man who was hit by a would-be assassin's bullet
just four weeks ago. Ronald Reagan is visibly thinner and frailer
but is walking easily under his own power.

Seventeen days earlier, Reagan returned to the White House to
recuperate. On April 16, he made his first public appearance since
his return and took a stroll around the Rose Garden with photographers in tow. The nation marveled at his vigor and quick recovery. Only Nancy knows that the event was carefully orchestrated to
reassure Americans that their seventy-year-old president was still
capable of leading the country.

The roar continues as Reagan strolls to the podium and shakes
hands with Vice President George H. W. Bush, who is president
of the Senate. Reagan also greets the rotund white-haired Speaker

of the House, Massachusetts representative Tip O'Neill. The president then turns to address the Congress.

But the ovation will not end.

Reagan grins. He is genuinely thrilled by the outpouring of warmth. His cheeks and forehead are red, thanks to hours spent enjoying the sun on the promenade outside the White House solarium. He wears a well-tailored dark blue suit with a blue striped tie. After three full minutes, the applause finally dies down, and Reagan begins his remarks.

Referring to the shooting, Reagan makes an unexpected joke: "You wouldn't want to talk me into an encore, would you?" Laughter erupts.

"Mr. Speaker, Mr. President," Reagan starts, "distinguished members of the Congress, honored guests, and fellow citizens: I have no words to express my appreciation for that greeting."

The purpose of the speech is to gain congressional approval for his economic recovery program. However, almost immediately, he detours away from the details of that plan to speak from the heart.

"I'd like to say a few words directly to all of you and to those who are watching and listening tonight, because this is the only way I know to express to all of you on behalf of Nancy and myself our appreciation for your messages and flowers and, most of all, your prayers, not only for me but for those others who fell beside me.

*[NEXT PAGES] President Reagan receives a standing ovation from members of Congress on April 28, 1981.* [Bettman/Corbis]

"The warmth of your words, the expression of friendship and, yes, love, meant more to us than you can ever know," Reagan tells America and the Congress. "You have given us a memory that we'll treasure forever. And you've provided an answer to those few voices that were raised saying that what happened was evidence that ours is a sick society."

# CHAPTER 36

# TIM McCARTHY

"Sick societies," Reagan continues, "don't produce young men like Secret Service agent Tim McCarthy, who placed his body between mine and the man with the gun simply because he felt that's what his duty called for him to do."

Agent McCarthy, the recipient of John Hinckley's fourth bullet, checked out of George Washington University Hospital on April 7. He will spend the rest of his life joking that the Devastator round ruined his new suit. But more important, the Secret Service will soon begin showing new agents videotape of the Reagan assassination attempt, pointing out how McCarthy shielded the president with his body in a linebacker crouch, arms and legs spread out. In doing so, Tim McCarthy exposed himself to the bullet. The round spun McCarthy as it entered the right side of his chest, knocking him to the ground. In a split second, the .22-caliber slug punctured a lung and passed through his diaphragm and liver before coming to rest against a rib. The surgery at George Washington to remove the bullet lasted a little more than an hour.

As Ronald Reagan speaks to Congress, Tim McCarthy has no regrets about what transpired. The father of two young children is a product of his rigorous training, and he is already making plans to get back on the job.

In this way, McCarthy and Ronald Reagan are two very similar Irishmen.

*Wounded Tim McCarthy, on the stretcher, is about to be loaded into the ambulance.*
[Associated Press]

# CHAPTER 37

# THOMAS DELAHANTY

"SICK SOCIETIES DON'T PRODUCE dedicated police officers like Tom Delahanty," Ronald Reagan tells Congress.

Officer Delahanty is considered an "exemplary officer" by his superiors, having received more than thirty commendations during his seventeen years on the force. Delahanty wasn't supposed to be at the Hilton on March 30. The forty-five-year-old Pittsburgh native usually worked with the K-9 Corps in Washington's downtown area.

But Delahanty's dog, Kirk, was recovering from heartworms. The dog lives with Delahanty and his wife, Jane, in suburban Maryland, and Delahanty left him home for the day. The officer accepted an assignment to work the Hilton detail instead.

Secret Service protocol stipulates that an agent never turn his back to a crowd when a president is present. But Tom Delahanty and the other D.C. police officers working the Hilton never received that training. This may have saved Delahanty's life. The bullet that went into his neck as he turned to gawk at President Reagan would have hit him in the throat had he been facing the shooter.

That is small solace for Delahanty. The bullet lodged in the lower left part of his neck, dangerously close to his spinal column. Doctors at Washington Hospital Center initially decided against removing the bullet, but upon learning days later that the Devastator might explode at any minute, they reversed their decision.

Delahanty was released from the hospital on April 11, but the Devastator has left its mark. Irreversible nerve damage to his left arm will force him to retire from the police department in November. Kirk will retire along with him and live out his days with Tom and his wife.

Even in retirement, the incident will haunt Officer Delahanty. The Secret Service will suggest that Hinckley could have been stopped. All it would have taken was for Delahanty and the other officers on the rope line to continue facing the crowd as Ronald Reagan departed the Hilton.

It is a question that will remain with Thomas Delahanty the rest of his life.

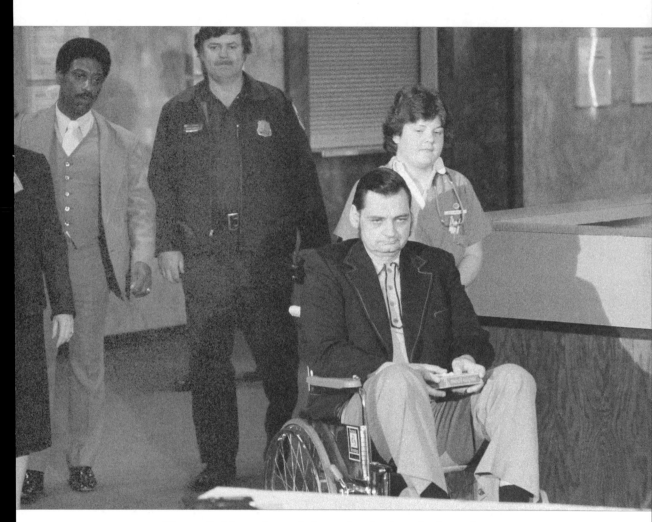

*Thomas Delahanty leaves the hospital twelve days after being shot.* [Associated Press]

# CHAPTER 38

# JAMES BRADY

RONALD REAGAN PAUSES FOR EMPHASIS. His eyes sweep the room. He is firmly in control of the speech. "Sick societies don't produce . . . able and devoted public servants like Jim Brady."

As Ronald Reagan speaks his name, Press Secretary James Brady lies in a bed at George Washington University Hospital, his head resting at a 20-degree angle to ease the pressure on his damaged brain.

Jim Brady is beginning a recovery process that will last a lifetime. The Bear, as Brady is called, was comatose when the Secret Service brought him to the hospital. Pieces of his skull were missing, and brain matter was visible. His eyes were swollen shut, and his breathing was rapid and shallow. Nerves were severed by the bullet's passage, and a blood clot was forming on his brain.

The trauma team cut off Brady's blue business suit and stashed it in a plastic bag beneath the gurney. A catheter was installed, as were intravenous lines to replenish fluid and blood. But it appeared to be

*James "The Bear" Brady, January 1981.* [Associated Press]

all for naught. James Brady's brain was swelling dramatically. Unless the swelling was stopped, it would squeeze the brain stem, which regulates the heartbeat and other vital functions of the body, through the bottom of the skull, and Brady would die.

But Brady was in luck. He was shot at a time of day when the hospital was at full staff—including a brain surgeon—allowing him immediate assistance. Within ten minutes, the trauma team had stabilized Brady enough to get him into a CT scan. However, the brain continued to swell, and the CT scan showed the dangerous blood clot forming; he needed surgery immediately.

But at 5:13 P.M., as word of Brady's grave condition leaked, Dan Rather of CBS News told America, "It is now confirmed that Jim Brady has died."

This was news to his wife, Sarah Brady.

It was also news to Dr. Arthur Kobrine, who led the surgical team then removing pieces of Brady's skull to relieve pressure on the brain.

Remarkably, the operation was a success. In another bit of luck, the blood clot had burst during surgery, creating a hole in the one area of the brain that is less important for a right-handed person like Brady. The potentially fatal pressure buildup immediately dropped, and Dr. Kobrine was able to reach the bullet. And though James Brady will remain in the hospital for many months, he is alive. Amazingly, he will eventually recover a great portion of his brain function.

James Brady is also now forcibly retired. For the rest of the Reagan administration, the individual taking his place will always be known as "acting" press secretary, out of respect for Brady.

# CHAPTER 39

# FINAL WORDS

Ronald Reagan is almost finished. "Sick societies don't make people like us so proud to be Americans and so very proud of our fellow citizens."

With those words, Reagan publicly puts the assassination attempt behind him.

"Now, let's talk about getting spending and inflation under control and cutting your tax rates."

//////////////////////////////////////////////////////////

# EPILOGUE

//////////////////////////////////////////////////////////

To some, it seemed that the world had undergone a major transition in the twenty-nine days between John Hinckley opening fire on March 30 and Ronald Reagan entering the chamber of the House of Representatives on April 28.

An exciting era in space travel had begun: astronauts John Young and Robert Crippen successfully piloted the new space shuttle on its inaugural voyage into the heavens. Launched April 12, 1981, twenty years to the day after Soviet cosmonaut Yury Gagarin became the first man in space, the shuttle *Columbia* forever changed manned spaceflight. It was revolutionary that *Columbia* could rocket into orbit and land back on Earth with wheels down, like a traditional airplane. Designed to transport people and cargo and dock with other orbiting craft such as satellites, the space shuttle was seen as the next step to people actually living and working in space and led

*Launch of the first STS (Space Transportation System),* Columbia. [Wikimedia]

★ 178 ★

*On April 5, 1982, President Reagan announced that he would address the United Nations on nuclear arms control. He invited Soviet president Leonid Brezhnev to do the same.* [Corbis]

to the development of the International Space Station. In the words of the National Aeronautics and Space Administration, the space shuttle "fundamentally changed our understanding of the universe."

And on April 24, with his long-delayed letter to Soviet leader Leonid Brezhnev, Reagan opened a new epoch of relations between the two nuclear superpowers. Reagan expressed a willingness to sit down at the negotiation table with Brezhnev, as the Soviet leader had demanded. However, Reagan also made it clear that "a great deal of tension in the world today is due to Soviet actions." He took Brezhnev to task for the Soviets' nuclear and military buildup, as well as his nation's ongoing attempts to directly and indirectly use force to increase its sphere of influence.

★ ★ ★

It was also during those days, and the ones that followed, that the national conversation turned to the attempted assassination. People asked how it could have happened. Had we not learned enough from the killings of John Kennedy, Robert Kennedy, Martin Luther King Jr., John Lennon, and the thousands of other people who are murdered in our country? How was it that the Secret Service failed to protect the president of the United States? How was it that John Hinckley was able to buy guns so easily, not once but repeatedly? And as the facts about Hinckley became known, some people questioned whether he was really insane. If not, why was it so easy for his lawyers to make the jury think he was?

April 7, 1981

Dear President Reagan

My students have expressed great concern about you and are pleased to hear about your rapid recovery.

Enclosed are cards that the students made for you, and we hope you will enjoy them.

Sincerely yours,
Mrs. Lorraine Buhrmann
Afternoon Kindergarten Class
Oakridge Elementary School

4/15/81

Dear Mrs. Buhrmann

Please convey my thanks to your students for their cards & letters and good wishes in my behalf. I am more grateful than I can say. I'm feeling better every day & much of that is due to the kindness of people such as the afternoon Kindergarten Class at Oakridge. Please know you have my heartfelt (over)

thanks.

Sincerely
Ronald Reagan

Rainwater caught the first of June will cure freckles.

Leslie Golocar

PRESIDENT REAgan
PLEASE gET BETTER
LOVE
KimAl en

Dear Kim — Forgive me for using your card for my answer but I wanted to let you know how very much I appreciate your good wishes & your lovely card.

Love Ronald Reagan

4/15/81

//////////////////////////////////////////////////////////

# AFTERWORD

//////////////////////////////////////////////////////////

## THE SECRET SERVICE

One thing was clear after the attempted assassination: it took only ten seconds to get President Reagan out of sight and securely in his limousine. Every analysis praised the Secret Service for its speed. But it was also clear that some aspects of the Secret Service's mandate to protect the president had to change.

The first thirty-nine presidents had customarily waved to crowds from close quarters, shook hands with groups of well-wishers, took questions from reporters on sidewalks, and used these moments of public exposure to polish their images.

The revised Secret Service protocol ended this pattern. Now tents are set up to shield the president from view when entering and leaving cars and buildings.

*Ronald Reagan received get-well cards from around the world. He sent answers back to many well-wishers.* [Ronald Reagan Library]

*President Reagan with Secret Service agents (left to right) Dennis McCarthy, Jerry Parr, Ray Shaddick, and Timothy McCarthy, July 31, 1981.* [Ronald Reagan Library]

It seems unbelievable today that until 1981, magnetometers were rarely used to scan people who would be close to a president. Now, even in large arenas, people are regularly scanned for firearms and other dangerous devices. John Hinckley was standing only fifteen feet away from Reagan; his gun would have been detected if the crowd had had to go through a screening gate.

Secret Service agents continue to be rigorously trained. The goal is to ensure that they react instinctively to threats—no thinking, no deciding, just well-planned and rehearsed action. Today, agents train for about two weeks every two months to reinforce and sharpen their skills.

## JERRY S. PARR

Jerry Parr, special agent in charge in the Secret Service's Presidential Protection Division, always said that he thought God was with him when he saved Ronald Reagan's life by shoving the president into the car and by changing the limo's destination from the White House to the hospital.

Four days after the attempted assassination, Jerry Parr wrote this letter to his team:

*April 3, 1981*
*SAIC Parr—PPD*
*The Events of March 30, 1981*
*All Personnel—PPD*

*The events of March 30, 1981, which we will never forget, are now a part of American History.*

*The pride and admiration I feel for each of you moves me deeply. All of our actions together in that incredible moment, were professional and instinctive. Training can only do so much. It takes a more profound motive to respond the way Tim McCarthy did. It was a response, self-sacrificial in nature, which all Americans in general, current and future agents in particular, will write about and think about for as long as this Agency exists.*

*Drew Unrue's instant response and skill in that drive to George Washington Hospital were instrumental in saving the President's life. Ray's quick move in helping me with the President, Dale's fast response to the follow-up car, Jim Varey's good judgment and assistance to Jim Brady, Eric's move toward the assailant, Bob's coverage of the departure, Kent's move toward the gun, Bill's excellent security arrangements, Dennis' skill at the wheel of the follow-up car, Russ Miller's quick decision to fill McCarthy's position, Mary Ann's good judgment in the motorcade, Bob Weakley's driving, and Joe Trainor in W-16\* who handled all of our emergency communications, were all performed in the very highest traditions of this Division.*

*Upon reflection, I believe the events of March 30 represent all that is worst in man and at the same time all that is best. Life is lived forward, but understood backward,*

*and in the many paths to maturity the loss of illusions is part of that most human process.*

*As each of us move apart physically in time from that terrible moment, we are forever bound together by the sound of gunfire and the sure and certain knowledge that, in the words of William Faulkner, we not only endured, but we prevailed.*

Jerry S. Parr
Special Agent in Charge

*Secret Service command post in the White House, directly below the Oval Office

*On April 23, 1981, Jerry Parr honors a Washington, D.C., mounted patrol officer for his service on the day of the assassination attempt.* [Ronald Reagan Library]

Nancy Reagan firmly credited Parr for saving her husband's life, and he continued to protect Reagan both at home and abroad. He retired from the service in 1985 and became a pastor. Parr died in 2015 at the age of eighty-five.

## JOHN WARNOCK HINCKLEY JR.

The man who shot Reagan remains at St. Elizabeths Hospital in Washington, D.C., a 160-year-old psychiatric facility. He resides in a fourth-floor room, eats in the cafeteria, attends therapy sessions, shoots pool, plays his guitar, and watches television. He can listen to any music he likes. There are no shackles on his wrists or ankles. But in this new life, he is not a free man.

A little more than a year after the shooting, Hinckley was still pining for Jodie Foster. He told the *New York Times* in a July 1982 letter: "My actions of March 30, 1981, have given special meaning to my life, and no amount of imprisonment or hospitalization can tarnish my historical deed. The shooting outside the Washington Hilton hotel was the greatest love offering in the history of the world. I sacrificed myself and committed the ultimate crime in hopes of winning the heart of a girl. It was an unprecedented demonstration of love. But does the American public appreciate what I've done? Does Jodie Foster appreciate what I've done?"

Hinckley continued: "I am Napoleon and she is Josephine. I am Romeo and she is Juliet. I am John Hinckley Jr. and she is Jodie Foster. The world can't touch us."

More than thirty years after being found not guilty of attempting to assassinate the president by reason of insanity, Hinckley may not remain at the hospital much longer. In December 2013, a federal judge declared he was "not a danger" and authorized visits of up to seventeen days at his mother's home in Williamsburg, Virginia. Hinckley is allowed to drive a car but not allowed to talk to the media. The Secret Service requires that Hinckley carry a GPS-enabled cell phone so agents can track his movements.

In January 2015, citing a legal doctrine that prevents defendants from being tried for the same issue in more than one criminal trial, prosecutors declined to press murder charges against Hinckley in the August 2014 death of James Brady, Reagan's press secretary. Brady's death had been ruled a homicide, as Hinckley's bullet directly caused the health issues that ultimately killed the press secretary at age seventy-three.

## RONALD WILSON REAGAN

Ronald Reagan was shot on the seventieth day of his first term as president. The following eight years were filled with triumph and a significant failure. He left office in 1989 and in 2004 died of pneumonia, complicated by Alzheimer's disease.

★  ★  ★

The letter that Reagan composed and sent to Leonid Brezhnev on April 24, 1981, was the first step in ending the Cold War. Rather than maintain a standoff, Reagan was forceful and vocal in dealing with the Soviets. One of his finest moments came in 1987 when he stood in front of the Berlin Wall, which divided free and communist Berlin, and called on Soviet leader Mikhail Gorbachev to "tear down this wall."

Reaganomics is the term still used for the government posture of tax cuts, reduced spending, deregulation, and controlled inflation. Reagan's economic policy bolstered the country and kept it in good shape until the early 1990s.

U.S. military power had decreased during the Carter years. Reagan increased spending by 40 percent to bring the country back up to superpower strength.

One of Reagan's primary goals as president was the reduction of nuclear arms in the world. His work laid the foundation for the first Strategic Arms Reduction Treaty, signed with the Soviet Union in 1991, which called for a 33 percent reduction in nuclear arms. A second round of talks with Russia two years later further reduced the amount to 50 percent.

Reagan was a strong proponent of the Strategic Defense Initiative, a plan to build a shield against a large-scale nuclear missile attack, in particular by the Soviet Union. He received criticism for wanting to build a system that would be so large, cutting edge, and expensive; later presidents phased out the program in favor of smaller, more targeted defenses. These systems have proven able to track and destroy a small-scale strike before an enemy missile reaches U.S. soil, as Reagan initially envisioned.

Reagan championed and signed the Canada–United States of America Free Trade Agreement, which eliminated tariffs for goods and services passing across the border.

*President Reagan and his Supreme Court justice nominee Sandra Day O'Connor pose on the grounds of the White House, July 15, 1981.* [Ronald Reagan Library]

The U.S. Supreme Court justices had always been men before Reagan's presidency. He promised to nominate the first woman to the court. The 99–0 confirmation of Sandra Day O'Connor in September 1981 was a groundbreaking achievement.

★   ★   ★

The Iran-contra affair grew out of Reagan's anticommunist and antiterrorism policies, including National Security Decision Directive 138, a top-secret plan to combat terrorism using "all available channels of communication . . . to persuade those now practicing or supporting terrorism to desist." Reagan affixed his signature to the directive on April 3, 1984.

Since 1980, Iran had been engaged in a fierce war with its neighbor Iraq and was desperate for weapons. Although the United States was publicly preventing arms sales to Iran, Reagan secretly authorized the sale of weapons in exchange for the release of Americans recently taken hostage by Iranian militants in the Middle East and to gain more influence in the region.

Some of the money from the arms sales was secretly funneled to contra guerrillas trying to oust the communist Cuba–backed Sandinista government in Nicaragua, despite Congress's ban at the time on using U.S. funds to support any fighting in that country.

The fallout of the scandal, after Reagan aides were fired or quit, resulted in a significant decrease in Reagan's job approval rating in the polls.

## NANCY DAVIS REAGAN

After leaving the White House, Nancy Reagan continued to champion the causes she focused on as first lady: the Foster Grandparents organization and drug education and prevention programs for children and young adults. The slogan developed for her prevention initiative, "Just Say No," has been widely adopted and is now shorthand for reminding children that they can choose to avoid drugs.

Following Ronald Reagan's death after suffering from Alzheimer's disease, Nancy Reagan worked tirelessly to lobby Congress to lift the federal restrictions on stem cell research, which could one day lead to a cure for the disease that robbed her of last years with her Ronnie. The Republican former first lady publicly thanked President Obama when he signed the stem cell bill in 2009, after George W. Bush had vetoed it twice during his tenure.

Nancy Reagan died on March 6, 2016, at her home in Los Angeles. She was ninety-four years old. She is buried next to her beloved husband at the Ronald Reagan Presidential Library in Simi Valley, California.

*Nancy Reagan speaks about the "Just Say No" campaign.* [Ronald Reagan Library]

# BEFORE POLITICS

A S A BOY, RONALD REAGAN was energetic and restless. He was born in Tampico, Illinois, on February 6, 1911. His mother was quite religious, and his father was a hard-drinking salesman. Their interactions, fueled by volatile natures, may be why Ronald Reagan avoided extreme behavior and sometimes seemed reserved.

Reagan did not do very well in school, struggling to maintain a C average in college. Though perhaps not a star student, he was a star on the football field and in the pool for the swim team. And he was busy in many areas of

*Ronald Reagan with his father, Jack; older brother, Neil; and mother, Nelle, about 1916.* [Mary Evans Picture Library]

college life—as a student council president and a member of the drama club. His ability to memorize paragraphs and repeat them back flawlessly was an asset both in the drama club and eventually in his acting career.

Reagan's first job after college was in radio, as a sportscaster for a station in Iowa, which led to a stint re-creating Chicago Cubs

*[RIGHT] Stars of the Eureka College football team in 1930. Ronald Reagan is on the far right.* [Mary Evans Picture Library]

*[BELOW] Ronald Reagan's childhood home in Dixon, Illinois.* [Library of Congress]

[*ABOVE*] *Ronald Reagan (front row, fourth from left) on his high school football team, 1925.* [Ronald Reagan Library]

[*LEFT*] *Publicity photo of Ronald Reagan as a young actor in the 1940s.* [Ronald Reagan Library]

baseball games on the air from live telegraph feeds. While he was covering the Cubs' spring training in California in 1937, Reagan took a movie screen test and received a seven-year contract from Warner Brothers. His salary was $200 per week.

Reagan's first marriage, to the actress Jane Wyman, ended in divorce. They had three children: Maureen; Michael, whom they adopted; and Christine, who was born four months premature and died after only a day.

*Ronald Reagan on his college swim team.* [Ronald Reagan Library]

# ALZHEIMER'S DISEASE

AFTER HIS PRESIDENCY, AS REAGAN settled into his role as senior statesman, his friends began to notice that his memory was sometimes less than clear. In 1994, he was diagnosed with Alzheimer's disease. The disease attacks the brain's nerve cells and increases in severity, beginning with loss of memory and eventually affecting language, thinking, and behavior. As the disease progressed, Reagan took a moment to write a typically gracious and heartfelt letter to the American people.

*November 5, 1994*

*My Fellow Americans,*

*I have recently been told that I am one of the millions of Americans who will be afflicted with Alzheimer's Disease.*

*Upon learning this news, Nancy and I had to decide whether as private citizens we would keep this a private* matter or whether we would make this news known in a public way.

In the past Nancy suffered from breast cancer and I had my cancer surgeries. We found through our open disclosures we were able to raise public awareness. We were happy that as a result many more people underwent testing. They were treated in early stages and able to return to normal, healthy lives.

So now, we feel it is important to share it with you. In opening our hearts, we hope this might promote greater awareness of this condition. Perhaps it will encourage a clearer understanding of the individuals and families who are affected by it.

At the moment I feel just fine. I intend to live the remainder of the years God gives me on this earth doing the things I have always done. I will continue to share life's journey with my beloved Nancy and my family. I plan to enjoy the great outdoors and stay in touch with my friends and supporters.

Unfortunately, as Alzheimer's Disease progresses, the family often bears a heavy burden. I only wish there was some way I could spare Nancy from this painful experience. When the time comes I am confident that with your help she will face it with faith and courage.

In closing let me thank you, the American people for giving me the great honor of allowing me to serve as your President. When the Lord calls me home, whenever that may be, I will

*leave with the greatest love for this country of ours and*
*eternal optimism for its future.*

*I now begin the journey that will lead me into the sunset*
*of my life. I know that for America there will always be a*
*bright dawn ahead.*

*Thank you my friends. May God always bless you.*

*Sincerely,*
*Ronald Reagan*

Reagan's condition deteriorated, and on June 5, 2004, he passed away at his home with his wife at his bedside.

Reagan's funeral was the largest since President Kennedy's. The National Cathedral in Washington, D.C., was filled with world leaders. Ronald Reagan is buried at his presidential library in Simi Valley, California, where his epitaph reads:

I KNOW IN MY HEART THAT MAN IS GOOD,

THAT WHAT IS RIGHT WILL ALWAYS EVENTUALLY

TRIUMPH, AND THERE IS PURPOSE AND WORTH

TO EACH AND EVERY LIFE.

*Nancy Reagan with her husband's coffin at his presidential library, where it lay in state before being flown to Washington, D.C., for the funeral.* [National Archives]

# GUNS AND GUN CONTROL

John Hinckley bought his first gun in 1979. The following year, he had three handguns. At the time, guns were sold at gun and pawn shops and through the mail. There were 160,000 gun dealers in the country in 1980. Some guns cost as little as $10. The buyer had to fill out a form stating that he or she was not a criminal, mentally unstable, or a drug addict. There was no waiting period; the buyer could walk out of the store with the gun immediately. The weapon Hinckley used in his assassination attempt came from a pawn shop.

At the time, checked baggage was not X-rayed, but when Hinckley sped out of Nashville, he did not have the chance to check his bag, so he tried to finesse his way through security with his carry-on and failed. In 1988, checked luggage began to be screened, but only on international flights. Since 2001, checked bags on all flights are screened.

*Evidence at John Hinckley's trial.* [Associated Press]

The gun control debate revolves around the Second Amendment to the U.S. Constitution: "A well regulated Militia, being necessary to the security of a free State, the right of the people to keep and bear Arms, shall not be infringed." Those who oppose gun control cite the Constitution. Those in favor say that the amendment was written when an armed citizenry was necessary and that such a time has passed.

After Reagan was shot, polls showed that the majority of Americans were overwhelmingly in favor of stronger gun control. James Brady and his wife, Sarah, became tireless advocates for the issue. In 1993, the Brady Handgun Violence Prevention Act created a five-day waiting period so that handgun purchasers' backgrounds could be checked against criminal records. Five years later, the National Instant Criminal Background Check System went into effect, ending the federal waiting period, and background checks were extended to the purchases of rifles and shotguns. After the September 11, 2001, terrorist attacks, the background checks began to include government terror watch lists, but people on a watch list are not prevented from buying a gun if they have no criminal record.

# GOVERNMENT WATCH LISTS

IN 1980, THE SECRET SERVICE had a computer file of four hundred individuals the agency considered most likely to attempt an assassination of the president; these were considered the most dangerous on a larger list of about twenty-five thousand who might be capable of such a killing. John Hinckley's name was not on either list, even though he had tried to smuggle guns aboard an airplane in Nashville and had been arrested for gun possession.

People who write threatening letters or e-mails to the president or other public officials are monitored by the Secret Service, FBI, and local law enforcement. The agencies can scan security feeds looking for stalkers, monitor public online sites for key words and phrases, follow up on tips, and access lists of people who are rejected for gun permits.

Today the FBI's Terrorist Screening Center in Virginia maintains a master list of people who are known or suspected to be involved in terrorist activities. Many government agencies nominate individuals for the list, and the information is shared with federal agencies dealing with aviation security, immigration and visa control, and domestic law enforcement. After the events of 9/11, national and international agencies are cooperating to ensure that what is known by one is shared with all.

# BY REASON OF INSANITY

On June 21, 1982, John Hinckley was found not guilty by reason of insanity on all thirteen counts brought against him for shooting President Reagan and three others. The jury of seven women and five men had deliberated for twenty-four hours over four days. They had heard eight weeks of testimony from forty-one witnesses—psychiatrists, medical doctors, ballistic experts, and others called by the prosecution and the defense.

The prosecution sought to prove that John Hinckley was lucid, was aware of the crime he would attempt, and made a conscious and rational choice to assassinate Reagan.

The defense cited Hinckley's delusion about his relationship with Jodie Foster, his history of decline, and his diagnoses of schizophrenia and other mental illnesses to prove that he could not be held responsible for his acts.

The jury decided for the defense. John Hinckley was taken to St. Elizabeths Hospital in Washington, D.C.

It is fair to say that the nation was shocked by the verdict. In the next several years, significant changes were made to laws governing the use of the insanity defense. A 1984 federal law more strictly defined the criteria for an insanity plea and shifted the burden of proof; the defense now has to prove by clear and convincing evidence that the defendant was insane, rather than the prosecution having to prove that the defendant was sane. Many states followed suit, and several went further, instituting verdicts of "guilty but mentally ill." Upon conviction the defendant would be sentenced to prison time but be entitled to receive mental health treatment. If the mental illness were to improve, the defendant would still have to serve out the prison term, unlike a defendant acquitted by reason of insanity, who must be released when it's determined he's no longer a danger to himself or others.

*St. Elizabeths Hospital, 1979.* [Library of Congress]

# TRANSFER OF POWER

THE SHOOTING OF RONALD REAGAN threw the transfer of presidential powers into the spotlight. At the time of the attempted assassination, Vice President Bush was in Air Force Two flying to Texas. Bush received a coded cable from Alexander Haig over the Teletype that the president was in serious condition and doctors were considering surgery, so after refueling in Austin, the plane headed back to Washington. Because there was no secure phone or radio communication between the aircraft and the White House, Bush could not take control of sensitive leadership issues.

If the vice president is not available to take charge, then according to the Constitution, the power passes to the Speaker of the House, who was Tip O'Neill. For a few hours, confusion consumed the White House. Responding to questions from the press about what was happening with an "I can't say," the official White House spokesman did not assuage the anxiety of the millions of people watching on television. Exasperated, Alexander Haig, the gruff retired four-star army general who was secretary of state, entered the press conference and publicly assumed control. Though illegal, his move showed a strong face to the public and to the Soviets, who were maneuvering submarines close to the East Coast.

The president's physician, who travels with the president both within the country and internationally, carries forms that a president can sign if he is about to undergo surgery or be otherwise incapacitated for hours or days. The presidential power passes to the vice president. In the fast-paced events in the emergency room at George Washington University Hospital, Dr. Ruge did not think of the forms. So even though Haig said he was in charge of the Situation Room, presidential power never officially left Reagan's hands.

*Vice President George H. W. Bush leads the regular cabinet meetings while President Reagan recovers in the hospital.* [Ronald Reagan Library]

# PRESIDENTIAL ASSASSINATIONS AND ATTEMPTS

**January 30, 1835: Andrew Jackson**

An unemployed house painter shot Jackson, but his gun misfired. Jackson turned around and beat him with his walking stick. The assailant spent the rest of his life in a mental institution.

**April 14, 1865: Abraham Lincoln***

John Wilkes Booth shot Abraham Lincoln while Lincoln was watching a play. Booth was a passionate supporter of the Southern cause during the Civil War.

**July 2, 1881: James Garfield***

A man who hoped to get a political appointment but was refused shot Garfield at a train station in Washington, D.C. Garfield died eighty days later of the wounds.

*Presidents who died as a result of their injuries

### September 6, 1901: William McKinley*

McKinley was shot twice in the chest by a man who thought the government was corrupt and ignored working men. One of the wounds became infected with gangrene and caused McKinley's death.

### October 13, 1912: Theodore Roosevelt (presidential candidate)

An unemployed man shot Teddy Roosevelt as he was about to give a speech. One of the bullets lodged in his chest, but Roosevelt made the speech anyway—even letting the audience know he had been shot.

### February 15, 1933: Franklin D. Roosevelt (president-elect)

A man shouting "Too many people are starving!" shot at Roosevelt as he was sitting in an open car in Miami. Roosevelt was not hit, but the mayor of Chicago, sitting near him, was killed.

### November 1, 1950: Harry S. Truman

In 1950, while the White House was being renovated, the president was living in the nearby Blair House. Two men who wanted Puerto Rico to be independent of the United States walked up the front steps. Guards challenged them, and shots were fired.

### November 22, 1963: John F. Kennedy*

Lee Harvey Oswald was arrested and charged for the shooting of the president as he traveled in an open car in a motorcade through Dallas. Oswald was shot two days later while he was being transferred to a secure jail cell.

## February 22, 1974: Richard Nixon

A man for whom a government agency had turned down a loan hijacked a plane, planning to crash it into the White House and kill the president. The would-be assassin killed himself during a standoff with law enforcement on the tarmac.

## September 5 and 22, 1975: Gerald Ford

Ford's first would-be assassin, Lynette "Squeaky" Fromme, hoped to impress convicted killer Charles Manson by shooting Ford. Secret Service agents wrestled her to the ground. Seventeen days later, a bystander foiled another assassination attempt by grabbing the assailant's arm.

## May 5, 1979: Jimmy Carter

Law enforcement officers were tipped off to an assassination attempt when they arrested a man with a starter pistol at a convention center where Carter was to speak. He confessed to working with two hit men hired to kill the president.

## March 30, 1981: Ronald Reagan

John Hinckley Jr. fired at and hit Reagan, hoping to win the attention of actress Jodie Foster. John Hinckley was the first presidential assailant since 1835 to be found not guilty by reason of insanity.

## April 14, 1993: George H. W. Bush (former president)

Bush was preparing to give a speech in Kuwait when a car filled with explosives was discovered. Sixteen terrorists were arrested.

### October 29, 1994: Bill Clinton

A man shot at people standing on the White House lawn. He hoped one of them was the president. The shooter was tackled by tourists who witnessed his actions.

### November 1996: Bill Clinton

While visiting the Philippines, Clinton escaped a bomb when it was discovered along his motorcade route; the route was changed.

### February 7, 2001: George W. Bush

A man shot at the White House while the president was inside. The would-be assassin was wounded by Secret Service agents.

### November 11, 2011: Barack Obama

A man with an assault rifle shot at the White House from outside the fence, leaving bullet marks on the facade. The president was not in the building at the time.

# THE PRESIDENTIAL MOTORCADE

On MARCH 30, 1981, RONALD REAGAN left the White House with the usual presidential motorcade. Even though it was only 1.3 miles to the Washington Hilton, the lineup included more than ten vehicles.

At the time, the Secret Service did not normally use decoy vehicles to shield the actual location of the president in the procession.

When Nancy Reagan traveled, her motorcade consisted of two cars.

Today, a presidential motorcade can have as few as ten or as many as forty cars, depending on the location and event. The vehicles include local police cars and motorcycles that clear the way, a decoy car, the president's car—still called Stagecoach—followed very closely by Halfback, which carries the president's Secret Service detail. There are also vehicles for electronic countermeasures, key staff, a military aide carrying the nuclear launch codes, and the president's doctor. Another van carries a counterassault team, and

an ID car has agents who are in constant contact with counter-intelligence teams. The largest van is the hazardous materials mitigation vehicle, with machines that can detect chemical and biological threats. Press vans follow, along with the White House Communications Agency van that provides for secure communication within the motorcade and with the outside world. An ambulance and more police cars bring up the rear.

A blood bank, with stores of blood of the president's type, and an oxygen supply are in the trunk of the vehicle the president is riding in.

When the president travels overseas, some of the cars and drivers travel with him.

[LEFT] *Motorcade cars usually travel with the president.* [National Archives]

[BELOW] *A presidential motorcade.* [Ronald Reagan Library]

# JELLY BEANS

IT IS WELL KNOWN THAT Ronald Reagan kept a jar of Jelly Belly jelly beans on his desk in the Oval Office. The tradition started when he was governor of California. He was trying to give up smoking a pipe and found that eating jelly beans helped, particularly those made by the Herman Goelitz Candy Company.

For Reagan's first inaugural, the company shipped two and a half tons of jelly beans to Washington. Red (very cherry), white (coconut), and blue (blueberry) jelly beans were given away as souvenirs at balls and placed in gift bags at dinners.

It is said that the president's favorite flavor was licorice.

*A full jar of jelly beans at the cabinet meeting conference table.* [Ronald Reagan Library]

# GALLERY OF REAGAN MOVIE POSTERS

WHEN DOCTORS ANALYZED REAGAN'S RECOVERY from the shooting, they often cited his excellent physique as the reason he did so well. As a Hollywood movie star, Reagan traded on his appearance; it was crucial to his popularity. After the assassination attempt, Reagan had a gym installed in the White House, which he used throughout his presidency, and he and Nancy tried to eat healthy food in small portions.

## A SELECTION OF RONALD REAGAN'S FILMS

Ronald Reagan appeared in more than fifty films. Here are some of his favorites.

### Dark Victory (1939)

Bette Davis plays a terminally ill heiress who falls in love with her doctor. Reagan plays her bar-hopping playboy friend.

### Code of the Secret Service (1939)

Reagan stars as an agent investigating the theft of Treasury banknotes. This film inspired nine-year-old Jerry Parr to pursue a career in the Secret Service.

### Knute Rockne—All American (1940)

In this film biography of the famous Notre Dame football player and coach, Reagan plays gridiron great George Gipp, who could run, pass, kick, and play defense. Gipp died of pneumonia shortly after the 1920 football season, for which he was named an All-American. In the movie, Gipp makes a deathbed request of Rockne: "Someday when the team is up against it . . . ask 'em to go in there with all they got and win just one for the Gipper." Reagan used that line many times in his campaigns.

### Kings Row (1942)

This melodrama of small-town life at the turn of the century may be Reagan's best film. He again plays a playboy, Drake, who dates the daughter of the town doctor but ultimately marries someone else. After Drake is injured in an accident, the doctor needlessly amputates his legs as retribution. Drake wakes up and asks, "Where's the rest of me?" Reagan used that line for the title of his 1965 autobiography.

### Desperate Journey (1942)

In this wartime action flick, Reagan and Errol Flynn star as airmen who crash behind German lines and struggle to return to England.

### Bedtime for Bonzo (1951)

As a college professor raising a baby chimp, Reagan gets spattered with oatmeal by Bonzo.

*Storm Warning* (1951)

Reagan plays a district attorney who tries to get the Ku Klux Klan out of his small town.

# CODE NAMES

Giving the president and the first family members code names is a relatively recent custom. As electronic communication became commonplace after World War II, both security and clarity suffered. Many communication lines, including telephones and radios, were not secure. And the voice quality could be poor or sporadic. Using a short, easily pronounced code name was efficient and effective. Here is a list of code names for presidents.

Harry Truman: *General* or *Supervise*

Dwight Eisenhower: *Providence* (*Scorecard* after he left office)

John Kennedy: *Lancer*

Lyndon Johnson: *Volunteer*

Richard Nixon: *Searchlight*

Gerald Ford: *Passkey*

JIMMY CARTER: *Deacon*

RONALD REAGAN: *Rawhide*

GEORGE H. W. BUSH: *Timberwolf*

BILL CLINTON: *Eagle*

GEORGE W. BUSH: *Trailblazer* (*Tumbler* before he was president)

BARACK OBAMA: *Renegade*

# PHOTOGRAPHING THE PRESIDENT AND FIRST FAMILY

IMAGES LIKE THE ONE on page 130 show sequences of photos capturing an event as it unfolds. The frames of the film are printed on a piece of paper called a contact sheet. Many contact sheets may be needed to show all the images taken at an event. If a newspaper wanted to publish a story about Mrs. Reagan's luncheon, for example, they might ask the White House for an image to accompany the story. The photograph office would look at the contact sheets and select the best images.

The border of the images on the contact sheets reads KODAK SAFETY FILM. This film was invented in the early 1900s to replace an older kind that had a tendency to catch fire. Eastman Kodak was the largest manufacturer of film and cameras in the 1900s. Its founder, George Eastman, wanted to make the camera "as convenient as the pencil." The Eastman Kodak Company is still in business, developing new ways of capturing and preserving images.

★ 225 ★

Every president has a staff of photographers, a chief official White House photographer, and his or her assistant photographers. Their job is to document the president's activities for the historical record and to provide images for the news media. These photographs record official travel, meetings, celebrations, speeches, and other important moments. A photographer may also capture more intimate, private moments in the life of a president and the family—and may even accompany them on vacations or to their private homes. First ladies and vice presidents also have photographers.

Presidential photographers may take up to 1,500 images a day.

The photographer who took most of the pictures of the assassination attempt on President Reagan was Ronald A. Edmonds, who was on the staff of the Associated Press. He won a Pulitzer Prize for spot news photography for those images. Although Michael Evans, the president's photographer, was also there, he was standing behind Reagan and did not have a good angle to capture the drama of the event.

*Cameras surround a president whenever they are in public.*
[Ronald Reagan Library]

# TIME LINE

**February 6, 1911**    Ronald Reagan is born in Tampico, Illinois.

**July 2, 1921**    Anne Frances Robbins is born in New York City. Known as Nancy, she is later adopted by her step-father, Loyal Davis.

**Summer 1926**    Reagan is hired as a lifeguard at Lowell Park, near his hometown, Dixon, Illinois. It is said he saved seventy-seven people from drowning in the Rock River in the seven summers he worked there.

**September 16, 1930**    Jerry Parr is born in Birmingham, Alabama.

**June 1932**    Reagan graduates from Eureka College in Illinois.

**December 1932**    Reagan lands a job in radio with WOC in Davenport, Iowa, first broadcasting football games and eventually re-creating Chicago Cubs baseball games from a telegraph feed.

**February 27, 1937**    Reagan enlists in the U.S. Army Reserve.

| | |
|---|---|
| **March 15, 1937** | Reagan makes a screen test for Warner Brothers studio while covering the Cubs' spring training in California. He signs a contract with the studio a month later. |
| **January 26, 1940** | Reagan marries actress Jane Wyman. |
| **October 5, 1940** | The movie *Knute Rockne—All American* is released, increasing Reagan's exposure. |
| **April 19, 1942** | Reagan is called up for active duty during World War II. Nearsighted, he is assigned to the motion picture unit in California, where he makes more than four hundred training films over the next three years. |
| **May 23, 1943** | Nancy Davis receives a bachelor's degree from Smith College in Massachusetts. |
| **1947** | Reagan has his first taste of politics as president of the Screen Actors Guild, a position he will hold until 1952 and then again in 1959. |
| **June 28, 1948** | Jane Wyman divorces Reagan; the split becomes final a year later. |
| **March 2, 1949** | Nancy Davis signs a seven-year contract with MGM Studios. |
| **July 1950** | Jerry Parr joins the U.S. Air Force military police. |
| **March 24, 1952** | Reagan marries Nancy Davis. |
| **May 29, 1955** | John Hinckley Jr. is born in Ardmore, Oklahoma. |
| **May 1962** | Jerry Parr graduates from Peabody College in Tennessee after accepting a job offer from the |

Secret Service; he begins work October 1 in the
New York field office.

**Fall 1962**  Reagan changes political parties, becoming a
Republican.

**October 27, 1964**  Reagan gives a televised speech in support of
presidential candidate Barry Goldwater and receives
national attention.

**1966**  Reagan runs for governor of California and wins in a
landslide.

**November 3, 1970**  Reagan is reelected governor.

**Fall 1973**  John Hinckley enrolls at Texas Tech.

**November 20, 1975**  Reagan announces his candidacy for president.

**February 8, 1976**  The movie *Taxi Driver* is released. John Hinckley
will see it fifteen times, forming an attachment to
young actress Jodie Foster.

**August 19, 1976**  Gerald Ford narrowly defeats Reagan for the
Republican nomination for president; Ford will lose
to Democrat Jimmy Carter in the national election
in November.

**August 26, 1979**  Jerry Parr becomes special agent in charge of the
Presidential Protective Division of the Secret Service.

**January 20, 1981**  Reagan is sworn in as the fortieth president of the
United States.

**March 30, 1981**  Reagan is shot by John Hinckley.

**April 28, 1981**  Reagan receives a standing ovation when he appears before Congress for the first time since the shooting.

**August 19, 1981**  Reagan nominates Sandra Day O'Connor to the U.S. Supreme Court; the Senate confirms her on September 21, by a vote of 99–0.

**June 21, 1982**  A jury finds John Hinckley not guilty by reason of insanity.

**January 20, 1985**  Reagan begins his second term as president.

**November 13, 1986**  Reagan goes on television to deny trading arms for hostages but admits that the United States sent "small amounts of defensive weapons and spare parts" to Iran and that Iran was expected to use its influence to get American hostages released. The scandal becomes known as the Iran-contra affair when Attorney General Edwin Meese discovers that money from the Iran arms sales was diverted to the contras fighting in Nicaragua.

**June 12, 1987**  In a speech at the Berlin Wall, Reagan demands, "Mr. Gorbachev, tear down this wall!"

**November 8, 1988**  George H. W. Bush, Reagan's vice president, is elected president, defeating Massachusetts governor Michael Dukakis.

**November 9, 1989**  The Berlin Wall comes down when, as part of a general loosening of the Eastern Bloc authoritarian system, East Germany announces that its citizens can visit West Germany. The fall of the wall paves the way for German reunification a year later.

| | |
|---|---|
| **November 5, 1994** | Reagan announces that he has Alzheimer's disease. |
| **June 5, 2004** | Ronald Reagan dies of pneumonia complicated by Alzheimer's disease at the age of ninety-three. |
| **October 9, 2015** | Jerry Parr dies of congestive heart failure at age eighty-five. |
| **March 6, 2016** | Nancy Reagan dies of congestive heart failure at the age of ninety-four. |

# THE AUTHOR RECOMMENDS . . .

## RECOMMENDED READING

### Ronald Reagan

Burgan, Michael. *Ronald Reagan*. New York: DK Publishing, 2011.

Milton, Joyce. *Who Was Ronald Reagan?* New York: Grosset & Dunlap, 2005.

Sutherland, James. *Up Close: Ronald Reagan*. New York: Viking, 2008.

### Secret Service

Butts, Ed. *Bodyguards! From Gladiators to the Secret Service*. Toronto: Annick, 2012.

Gaines, Ann. *The U.S. Secret Service*. Philadelphia: Chelsea House, 2000.

Seidman, David. *Secret Service Agents: Life Protecting the President*. New York: Rosen, 2003.

### Vietnam War

Caputo, Philip. *10,000 Days of Thunder: A History of the Vietnam War*. New York: Atheneum, 2005.

Sheinkin, Steve. *Most Dangerous: Daniel Ellsberg and the Secret History of the Vietnam War*. New York: Roaring Brook, 2015.

**Watergate**

Cohen, Daniel. *Watergate: Deception in the White House.* Brookfield, CT: Millbrook, 1998.

Kilian, Pamela. *What Was Watergate?* New York: St. Martin's, 1990.

**1980s**

Corrigan, Jim. *The 1980s Decade in Photos: The Triumph of Democracy.* Stockton, NJ: Enslow, 2010.

Torr, James D., ed. *The 1980s.* San Diego: Greenhaven, 2000.

# RECOMMENDED VIEWING

*The American Presidents 1945–2010: Postwar & Contemporary United States.* Disney Educational Productions, 2010. DVD, 80 minutes. Ages 8–14.

*The Reagan Revolution.* Learn Our History, 2012. DVD, 60 minutes. Ages 8–14.

# BIBLIOGRAPHY

O'Reilly, Bill, and Martin Dugard. *Killing Reagan: The Violent Assault That Changed a Presidency.* New York: Henry Holt, 2015.

Parr, Jerry, and Carolyn Parr. *In the Secret Service: The True Story of the Man Who Saved President Reagan's Life.* Carol Stream, IL: Tyndale House, 2013.

Reagan, Nancy, and William Novak. *My Turn: The Memoirs of Nancy Reagan.* New York: Random House, 1989.

Wilber, Del Quentin. *Rawhide Down: The Near Assassination of Ronald Reagan.* New York: Henry Holt, 2011.

# SOURCE NOTES

WHEN RESEARCHING A CONTEMPORARY FIGURE, we are fortunate to be able to watch and listen to that person on film. On the Internet you can see Ronald Reagan the actor, Ronald Reagan the president, and Ronald Reagan the senior statesman. Press conferences, inaugurations, speeches, debates, interviews, and much more are available online. In addition, we consulted books, magazines, archives, newspapers, FBI and CIA files, online databases, and transcripts of interviews with people who worked with the Reagans.

The Ronald Reagan Presidential Foundation and Library (reaganfoundation.org) contains biographical information, his official White House diary, a vast visual archive, and commentary about our fortieth president.

To see where Reagan spent his years as president, visit the White House Museum (whitehousemuseum.org) for a visual tour of that magnificent building through the years.

Jerry Parr and his wife, Carolyn, wrote a stirring memoir of his time in the Secret Service called *In the Secret Service: The True Story of the Man Who Saved President Reagan's Life*. He also gave interviews in which he described the events and aftermath.

# INDEX